To

_____

From

_____

Message

_____

_____

_____

One-Minute Devotions for Women

© 2004 Christian Art Gifts, RSA
      Christian Art Gifts Inc., IL, USA

Designed by Christian Art Gifts

Printed in China

ISBN 978-1-86920-140-1

10 11 12 13 14 15 16 17 18 19 – 29 28 27 26 25 24 23 22 21 20

ONE-MINUTE DEVOTIONS

FOR WOMEN

Carolyn Larsen

christian
art gifts®

JANUARY

*New Perspective
on Your Priorities*

Life Plans

"For I know the plans I have for you," declares
the LORD, *"plans to prosper you and not to
harm you, plans to give you hope and a future."*
Jeremiah 29:11

Great news – you are not free-floating. There is a plan for your life, even if you don't know what it is at the moment. God's plan may not be the same as your plan, but as you assess various situations and set priorities as to how you spend your time, energy and money, you definitely want to get in touch with what God wants for you.

It's comforting to know that He is involved in your life and cares about what you do and how you spend your time. He isn't trying to hide His plan from you, but you will need to exert some effort to discover it. Spend some time with God asking for His direction and guidance.

Time to Praise

*It is good to praise the LORD and make music
to your name, O Most High, to proclaim your
love in the morning and your faithfulness at night.*
Psalm 92:1-2

It's always good to take into consideration what God wants when you are setting priorities. One thing we know He wants is our praise. Do you set aside time in your day to spend with God? In that quiet time do you praise Him? Or are your prayers filled with requests, fears or complaints? Make a point to set aside time to praise God for who He is and what He has provided for you.

Focus your thoughts on praise and remember His faithfulness to you. More than likely your day will go better and you will find that your attitude is improved.

Important versus Urgent

He who is kind to the poor lends to the LORD,
and he will reward him for what he has done.
Proverbs 19:17

How do you spend your time? You may say that certain things are important to you, such as helping others by donating time to a food pantry or shelter. But if you don't actually do those things, then they aren't really that important to you.

As you set priorities in your life, it's important to act on them, not just write them down on a list. Quite often in life, the important things get pushed aside by things that shout for your attention, even if they aren't really that important. Be careful to set priorities worthy of your time and calling from God, and to put those priorities into action.

Family Goals

*But as for me and my household,
we will serve the LORD.*
Joshua 24:15

It has often been said that the attitude of the wife/
mother in the home sets the attitude for everyone
else in the home. "If the momma isn't happy –
nobody is happy." It is also worth considering that
the priorities set by the wife/mother have a direct
influence on those of the rest of the family, too. If
you, as wife or mother, decide that it is important
for you to serve God, it will make a real difference
in your family and the relationship they have with
the Lord.

Meet the challenge and set priorities that will
provide the opportunity and atmosphere for the
rest of your family to make God important in
their lives.

Striving for Excellence

Whatever you do, work at it with all your heart, as working for the Lord, not for men.
Colossians 3:23

Slipshod isn't a word you hear much anymore. There are more modern ways of describing a person's mediocre efforts to complete an obligation or finish a job. For a believer who is representing the Lord Jesus Christ in all she does, slipshod efforts are not an option.

Make it a priority to do a job with all your heart, to the best of your ability. Present your efforts to the Lord as part of your praise to Him for the abilities and talents He has given you. Make excellence a priority in your life. Don't settle for less. Your efforts will be noticed by those around you and will be a positive testimony of your walk with the Lord.

Constant Trust

*Trust in him at all times, O people; pour
out your hearts to him, for God is our refuge.*
Psalm 62:8

Do you set New Year's Resolutions? Sometimes it's helpful at the beginning of a new year to list the things that are important goals for the new year – priorities to work on. Of course, realistically many of them will fall by the wayside before January is over, but sometimes one or two stick.

One priority to work on is trusting God – all the time. Learning to trust Him to the point that you can pour out your heart to Him, with all your pain, pleading, and joy ... and know that He hears you. He cares, and you can find shelter in Him any time.

Number One Priority

*"Any of you who does not give up
everything he has cannot be my disciple."*
Luke 14:33

This verse is pretty convicting when you think about it in relation to setting goals or priorities. Jesus says that you must give up *everything* in order to be His disciple. That makes the priority setting easy, doesn't it?

Being Christ's disciple must be first – before any other responsibilities, desires or even priorities. It must be the filter through which all other things are viewed. Once the priority of giving everything up for God is established, then all other priorities fall in line behind this one that is the standard.

Nothing is more important than your walk with God and growth in Him. If other things don't enhance that one goal, then they don't belong on your list of priorities. Simple, isn't it?

Ultimate Choice

For to me, to live is Christ and to die is gain.
Philippians 1:21

For a Christian, nothing is more important than knowing Christ and living for Him. Nothing is more important than showing others what Christ is like, by the way you live your life. This doesn't happen by accident. Every day you make choices about how you will behave, how you will relate to other people, what your actions and reactions will be. Every day you choose over and over whether or not you will live for Christ.

The last part of this verse puts life in perspective. As you make these constant choices, you are also choosing your place in eternity. A Christian believes with all her heart that living for Christ is important, and that dying brings with it the promise of a great reward – being with Christ forever. That puts the things of this world in perspective, doesn't it?

All or Nothing

*You will seek me and find me when
you seek me with all your heart.*
Jeremiah 29:13

No half-hearted goal setting allowed! If knowing God, living for Him, and growing in your faith is important, then it's worth giving your whole heart to it. You can put on a fancy show for other people and convince them that you're doing a good job of seeking to know God better. However, the bottom line is that you can't fool God. He looks deep into your heart and knows whether your efforts to know Him are shallow or whether they run deep.

If they are deep and your heart's desire is to know Him with all your heart, then mistakes and failures will be brushed aside. God cares about what your heart's priority is.

Looking Forward

*One thing I do: Forgetting what is behind
and straining toward what is ahead, I press on
toward the goal to win the prize for which God
has called me heavenward in Christ Jesus.*
Philippians 3:13-14

A very important guideline for setting priorities is to keep looking forward. Learn from past experiences and mistakes, but don't continue looking backward at them. Look forward to experiences that will help you continue to grow to a deeper level of faith in Christ Jesus. The things you give your time and energy to should help you become a better person and a stronger Christian.

Don't beat yourself up over past failures. Forget them and turn to look at what is ahead for you. Face the finish line and do everything you can to be worthy of the prize you will receive when you cross that line.

Foundational Trust

Blessed *is the man who trusts in the*
LORD, *whose confidence is in him.*
Jeremiah 17:7

Where have you put your trust? Who do you depend on? As you think about setting priorities and goals it is good to start with your foundation. Some people put their trust in other people, completely relying on their opinions. Some put their trust in material things and don't feel successful or important unless they have more possessions than others. Some put their trust in careers or even unhealthier things such as drugs and alcohol. The only sure foundation is Jesus Christ. If your trust is in Him you will never be disappointed because He is worthy of your confidence.

Make it a priority to place your confidence where it should be, firmly rooted in Jesus Christ.

Hidden Life

*Set your minds on things above,
not on earthly things. For you died, and
your life is now hidden with Christ in God.*

Colossians 3:2-3

Life is so busy. You may find that your mind is usually racing to keep track of all the things you need to do. Multi-tasking means multi-thinking. While it's certainly important to keep life going, particularly if you have a family who is depending on you to do so, it is even *more* important to focus your thoughts on things above.

Paul points out here that, when you became a believer, you died and the meaning and purpose of your new life is hidden with Christ in God. So, to learn about that life and to grow deeper in Him, requires focusing your thoughts on Him. The better you know Christ, the more you will understand about your life.

Seed Planting

*A man reaps what he sows. The one who sows
to please his sinful nature, from that nature
will reap destruction; the one who sows to please
the Spirit, from the Spirit will reap eternal life.*

Galatians 6:7-8

Even a novice gardener knows that you must plant
corn if you want to grow corn. You won't grow corn
if you plant squash seeds ... no matter how much
you wish or pray for corn.

This directly relates to life priorities. If you spend
your energy in selfish, sinful ways, you'll not be
pleasing God. You can pray for spiritual growth,
pray for God to work in your life and ask Him to
help you through problems, but your prayers won't
do much good. You must do your part. If you want
to please Him and grow in Him, then spend time
reading His Word and learning about Him.

Focused on God

*Whom have I in heaven but you? And earth has nothing
I desire besides you. My flesh and my heart may fail, but
God is the strength of my heart and my portion forever.*

Psalm 73:25-26

The psalmist knew that life on this earth has nothing
to offer that can compare with God. Riches, success,
health and fame will all fall away in time. Only God
will stand the test of time.

You can be certain that Satan will constantly
attack your efforts to make God the strength of
your heart. Because of his persistence, you must
make a conscious choice every day to put God at
the forefront of your heart and life. Satan will toss
many distractions in front of you to attempt to turn
you away from God. Don't let him. Learn from the
psalmist and stay focused on God.

Well-Placed Hope

*Those who hope in the L*ORD *will*
renew their strength. They will soar on
wings like eagles; they will run and not grow weary,
they will walk and not be faint.
Isaiah 40:31

Do you long for victory in your life? We all want relief from the stresses that weigh us down. We long for freedom and strength to keep on going. The pathway to that kind of life is found in this verse – put your hope in the Lord.

God will supply the strength you need to get through life. His energy will keep you going, and, while you may tire physically, you will be revitalized emotionally and spiritually. How do you put your hope in the Lord? Make spending time with Him a priority each day. Read His Word, be quiet before Him and wait for Him to speak to your heart.

Contentment

*Keep your lives free from the love of money and be
content with what you have, because God has said,
"Never will I leave you; never will I forsake you."*
Hebrews 13:5

This is a tough assignment in our world today. The world measures success by the accumulation of money, which leads to influence and power.

God measures success in a different way. He encourages you to keep the love of money off your list of priorities. Satan will continually subtly nudge you to desire more and more money, more and more things. God encourages you to remember that what really counts is His presence in your life. He promises to be with you always in all ways. So make it a priority to know Him better and better. That means your priorities won't be focused on money, but will be focused on spiritual things.

Choose Well

*How much better to get wisdom than gold,
to choose understanding rather than silver!*

Proverbs 16:16

If you page through many popular magazines you will see that the world puts much importance on money. The more money you have the more successful you are perceived to be.

Books and articles are written on how to get more of it and how to spend what you have. The temptation is to make money the number one priority of your life, and all other priorities grow from that one. But there are things that are really so much more important than money. Wisdom and understanding should rank higher than money. Wisdom and understanding will have a deeper impact on what kind of person you are and that will leave a more lasting legacy with your friends and family.

Who's Number Two?

*Do nothing out of selfish ambition or
vain conceit, but in humility consider
others better than yourselves. Each of you
should look not only to your own interests,
but also to the interests of others.*
Philippians 2:3-4

A Christian youth camp used to give an award
every summer to the camper who best lived out
the theme *Jesus first, others next, self last.* They
encouraged young people to always put Jesus first
in their lives. Knowing Him and obeying Him was
to be their number one priority.

The number two priority they encouraged is
sometimes a little harder: considering the desires
and needs of other people over your own. This
verse is a flashback to Jesus' words that real love
means laying down your life for a friend. Serving
others should truly be important to you.

Giving Back

Each of you must bring a gift in proportion to the way the Lord your God has blessed you.
Deuteronomy 16:17

Some people are fine with the instructions to worship God, pray to Him, or study His Word, but when giving is mentioned, their ears close up. They live by the philosophy, "What's mine is mine and what God gives me is mine." The instruction in this verse was given to the Israelites at the first Passover and the theme is repeated many times throughout Scripture. So, it must be important for us, too.

God has blessed us and He expects us to give back to Him a portion of that blessing. Our giving shows that we understand that all we have is a gift from Him and that we care about His Word being spread throughout the world. Giving isn't a suggested priority – it's a commanded priority.

True Faith

*We have come to share in Christ if we hold firmly
till the end the confidence we had at first.*
Hebrews 3:14

Holding firmly to your faith is the priority here. How does your faith hold up under the stress of unemployment, marriage problems, rebellious children, broken friendships, or health issues? That's where the rubber meets the road. It's easy to have faith when everything is going well. But when trouble comes ... and sticks around ... how does your faith hold up?

True faith is constant, it doesn't roll in and out depending on the situation. It stays focused on Christ and holds on to Him tenaciously. Focus your heart on Christ and strive to know Him better and better.

Learn to trust Him ... no matter what.

Choose Your Path

*Blessed is the man who does not walk in
the counsel of the wicked or stand in the
way of sinners or sit in the seat of mockers.
But his delight is in the law of the LORD,
and on his law he meditates day and night.*
Psalm 1:1-2

You have the freedom to choose the direction of
your life. You can choose to follow those who try
to influence you to live your life outside the realm
of obedience to God, those who care nothing about
Him or His values.

Or you can choose to obey God's law and spend
your time with others who also love Him.

It's a better choice to surround yourself with
friends who want to know God in a deeper way.
Together you can encourage one another, study His
Word, and hold one another accountable in your
walk with Him.

Serving Whom?

I care very little if I am judged by you or by any human court; indeed, I do not even judge myself. My conscience is clear, but that does not make me innocent. It is the Lord who judges me.
1 Corinthians 4:3-4

For whom do you live your life? Does the approval of people around you determine the choices you make and the path you follow? It shouldn't. As you set priorities in your life, one of the most important things you must realize is that the only person who has any right to judge you is God. Pleasing Him should be the most important thing in your life. That really sets you free – because you wouldn't be able to please all the people around you all the time anyway, but if you serve God then those around you should also be pleased with you.

Love

"A new command I give you: Love one another. As I have loved you, so you must love one another. By this all men will know that you are my disciples, if you love one another."
John 13:34-35

Do you love other people? No, really love them, not just enjoy being around them. These verses aren't talking about a surface relationship where you casually ask a friend how things are going but then change the subject before she responds.

Jesus said that we should love one another in the same way He loves us. That means sacrificial love – putting others' needs before your own and actively looking for ways to serve others. It means giving, giving, giving. It means flat out, bottom line, all the way loving.

That is the kind of love that will show Christ's love to others.

God's Word

*We must pay more careful attention therefore, to
what we have heard, so that we do not drift away.*

Hebrews 2:1

It seems that we are constantly being bombarded
with information. The internet, the media, your job
and people around you are continually dumping
information on you. That makes it difficult to stay
focused on what is truly important.

The preaching and teaching of God's Word
should be of primary importance to you. In fact,
you may say that it is, but with all the information
blitzing your mind, the truths of God's Word can
sometimes get pushed aside.

Be careful not to let that happen. Keep the teachings of God's Word in the center of your mind so
you don't drift away from them.

Real Treasure

"Do not store up for yourselves treasure on earth, where moth and rust destroy, and where thieves break in and steal. But store up for yourselves treasures in heaven."
Matthew 6:19-20

When you come to the end of life on this earth it's not going to matter how many pairs of shoes you own, how much square footage your house has, what kind of car you drive, or even how many letters are behind your name. It just doesn't matter what you accumulate on this earth. This life is a pass-through to a better place.

Oh, you should enjoy life, but don't focus on accumulating worldly successes. Use this life to lay up treasures in heaven by loving and serving God and loving and serving others. That's the treasure that will ultimately make a difference.

Who's Number One?

You, my brothers, were called to be free. But do not use your freedom to indulge the sinful nature; rather, serve one another in love.

Galatians 5:13

The world tells us that our number one priority should be ourselves. "Watch out for number one!" The world says that if you don't take care of yourself, no one else will either. It has a "You're on your own" mentality.

But Scripture doesn't teach that. Scripture says we should serve one another. You can't make yourself number one and still serve others. You must put yourself on the back burner in order to serve others. Is that a priority in your life? Do you desire to help others in any way you can? Do you do that with love and no resentment? If so, you are well on the way to being the person God wants you to be.

Real Wisdom

Who is wise and understanding among you?
Let him show it by his good life, by deeds
done in the humility that comes from wisdom.
James 3:13

Who doesn't want to be considered wise? No one sets out to be a fool. The evidences of wisdom are outlined here as deeds done in humility. This means doing good deeds without a "hooray for me" attitude.

Humble people do not need to call attention to themselves, do not always need to be number one. They enjoy helping others succeed and grow.

A person can brag about her wisdom and understanding, but if it isn't shown by the way she lives, then it probably isn't real wisdom and understanding. These qualities cannot be faked for the long term. Make it a priority to ask God to develop wisdom and understanding in your life.

Daily Praise

Praise the LORD. Praise the LORD,
O my soul. I will praise the LORD all my life;
I will sing praise to my God as long as I live.
Psalm 146:1-2

When it comes to setting priorities in life, what could be more important than praising God? Now, it might seem that this is an unnecessary priority to mention. After all, who would dare say that we shouldn't praise God? But how often does praise for God get lost among all the requests we make of Him? How often does the praise get lost in puddles of disappointment when He doesn't do what we think He should do?

Make it a priority to push aside all the requests, and just praise Him for who He is. Enjoy all that He does for you. Praise Him every day. Doing so will help your attitude!

Priority Adjustment

Command those who are rich in this present
world not to be arrogant nor to put their
hope in wealth, which is so uncertain, but to
put their hope in God, who richly provides
us with everything for our enjoyment.
1 Timothy 6:17

There is nothing wrong with being wealthy ... God blesses some people with an abundance of material things. The problem comes when a person begins to trust her wealth more than she trusts God. If you have been blessed with material possessions and wealth, you should make it a priority to regularly examine where your hope is.

Look at what you truly depend on – deep down in your heart – to get you through the hard times. If you're not trusting God with everything else, then you need to readjust your priorities. Only God can be completely depended on. Only God will never change.

CAROLYN LARSEN

JANUARY 30

Immovable Heart

My heart is steadfast, O God, my heart is steadfast.
Psalm 57:7

What image does the word *steadfast* bring up in your mind? You probably think of something completely immovable. Something that stands firm, not budging an inch, no matter what. Something that holds on so tenaciously that even a powerful wind can't blow it away.

That's the way your heart should be connected to God. Steadfastly attached to Him – nothing, absolutely nothing should be able to break the relationship. Your heart should be buried in God, no matter what problems or trials come your way. This doesn't just happen. It is a minute by minute decision to walk away from evil and turn to God. That makes it a life-choice priority. Be steadfast in Him!

Live to Serve

*Serve wholeheartedly, as if you
were serving the Lord, not men.*
Ephesians 6:7

It is nice to be served. It feels special to have someone wait on you and take care of your every need – the way you imagine very wealthy people or royalty live every day. However, reality is probably that you are only served at a restaurant (not the kind where your dinner is wrapped in paper!).

This verse is a good reminder that it is nice to be served. We can bring joy to others by serving them. When we put someone else's needs above our own desires and conveniences, we are living out the sacrificial love of Jesus.

An old acronym explains this: JOY. Serve Jesus, Others, You. Make it your priority to serve Jesus, serve others, and put yourself at the bottom of the list.

FEBRUARY

Parenting Can Be a Pleasure

Loving Discipline

He who spares the rod hates his son, but he who loves him is careful to discipline him.

Proverbs 13:24

Children don't seem to understand the truth of the sentence, "This hurts me more than it does you." In fact, this idea has become a gag for comedians to use. But in reality it's true, isn't it? It's no fun for parents to discipline their children. Parents don't look forward to discipline with a "Yahoo, I get to ground the kid!" attitude.

But discipline is necessary. It sets guidelines for children so they know where the boundaries are. Children like to know where the lines are for what is acceptable and what isn't. Of course, discipline should be firm, consistent, and given in love. That's how God disciplines His children. There couldn't be a better example to follow!

Consistency

*Fathers do not exasperate your
children; instead, bring them up in the
training and instruction of the Lord.*
Ephesians 6:4

Whew! Moms are off the hook with this verse ... not! While Paul specifically mentioned fathers in this verse, it's unreasonable to think that a mom can parent any way she wants but only fathers have to be careful not to frustrate the children.

What kinds of things might frustrate or exasperate a child? Inconsistency in disciplining them could be a major thing. If an action brings discipline one day, but not the next, children will be confused about what is proper behavior. Be careful to be consistent in discipline.

Make every effort to teach your children what is right and wrong from God's perspective. Instill in them an understanding of what it means to live for the Lord.

Daily Life

Impress [these commandments] on your
children. Talk about them when you sit
at home and when you walk along the road,
when you lie down and when you get up.

Deuteronomy 6:7

Do your children see consistency between the "Sunday Morning Mom" and the "Thursday Afternoon Mom"? In other words, can your children see you living out the Christian life in front of them? Or do they see two different moms – one that takes them to Sunday school and sings hymns in church and listens to the sermon – and one who shows no evidence of God's presence in her life the rest of the week?

Make God's Word an obvious presence in your life so that all week long you live it and speak it. That way your children will see the relevance of God's Word to everyday life. That is a great lesson to give your children.

Honoring Parents

Honor your father and your mother,
so that you may live long in the
land the LORD your God is giving you.
Exodus 20:12

What kind of example do you set for your children? Do you honor your parents or do your children hear you complaining about and criticizing your parents? Your children will develop their pattern of how to treat parents as adults by the way they observe you treating yours.

Do you think that your parenting skills are much better than your parents' skills? Do you feel that you relate to your children much better than your parents related to you ... that your children will always love to have you around and value your opinions? Well, maybe ... hopefully. Make every effort to honor your parents so that your children learn to do the same.

Model Lives

*Don't let anyone look down on you because
you are young, but set an example for the believers
in speech, in life, in love, in faith and in purity.*
1 Timothy 4:12

Rodney Dangerfield might say that kids get no respect. One reason for that is because of kids who make immature decisions, who behave poorly, and just generally don't show that they are trustworthy. Help your children understand that. Teach them to make wise decisions and to live their lives in a way that shows good judgment and discernment. Encourage your children to live their lives showing love to those around them.

As they live in this way they will be an example to those around them – young and old!

Lead with Love

The LORD is gracious and compassionate,
slow to anger and rich in love.
Psalm 145:8

What kind of temper do you have? Do you store up your frustrations, then explode over some silly "straw that breaks the camel's back"? Do you react immediately when you're upset so that your children fear your anger? Are you fairly controlled and able to handle situations with composure?

The Lord is a good example for all parents. He understands where His children are coming from. He cares about the situations that make us behave the way we do. He understands our emotions. He takes a long time to get angry and His discipline is always couched in love. That's a good example for any parent – lead with love.

Hard Work!

All hard work brings a profit,
but mere talk leads only to poverty.

Proverbs 14:23

You don't want your child to be all talk. You know people like that who talk a good career, a prosperous future, big plans and dreams; but they actually accomplish very little in life. They don't want to actually get their hands dirty, work up a sweat and *work*.

A good lesson to teach your children is that the only way to get ahead in life is to work … hard. Model this for them by having a good work ethic and not backing away from hard work. Let your children work right along beside you in the house or the yard. Be patient with them as you teach them the right way to do jobs and encourage pride in a job well done. You'll be teaching them an important life lesson.

Best Behavior

Be patient with everyone.
1 Thessalonians 5:14

Why is it that we often have less patience with our own family members than with anyone else? We put on our best behavior when we walk outside our homes, but when we come home our patience and understanding sometimes seems to disappear. Perhaps we feel safe at home; like we can truly be ourselves and we don't have to worry about what family members think of us. We feel confident that they will love us, no matter what.

However, our family members – the people we love the most in the world – deserve the best treatment, the most patience, love, and understanding we can give them. Scriptures encourage us to show this kind of behavior to everyone. Being an example of God's love to our own children is a privilege we shouldn't take lightly.

Living Example

*Take to heart all the words I have
solemnly declared to you this day, so that
you may command your children to
obey carefully all the words of this law.*
Deuteronomy 32:46

It is quite a responsibility to teach your children to take seriously the command to obey God. Moses understood the seriousness of this command. He knew that we can't really preach obedience to our children if we are not doing our best to obey God's commands ourselves. Our lives will speak louder than our words. Children are very quick to see inconsistencies.

Take God's teachings to heart, make them a vital part of your life so that your instructions and guidance to your children will have substance. Let them see that you live what you teach.

A Humble Child

*Whoever welcomes a little child
like this in my name welcomes me.*
Matthew 18:5

Jesus' disciples were wondering which of them would be most important in Heaven. Jesus must have shocked them when He called a child to come and stand in their midst, and then spoke these words. He focused their attention on how important children are. They are not to be pushed aside as unimportant.

Welcoming a child is like welcoming Jesus. Caring for children, loving them, teaching them, training them is important. Jesus shut down the disciples' prideful struggle to claim importance. He pointed out the humility of a child and the purity of a child's love.

This is a good reminder for us to focus on children – teach them and learn from them at the same time!

It's Okay to Cry

*There is a time for everything ... a time
to weep and a time to laugh,
a time to mourn and a time to dance.*
Ecclesiastes 3:1, 4

Has your child seen you cry? Has your child, especially your son, seen his father cry? Sometimes life is hard, pain comes into all our lives. It is a privilege for a parent to be able to teach her children how to handle all of life's experiences. If your children see you grieve and cry when the situation calls for such emotion, it gives them the freedom to experience those same emotions.

It's especially important for your son to know that men can cry without their manhood being threatened. Teach your children about the vicissitudes of life and give them the freedom to express the appropriate emotions for each situation.

Guidelines

I gain understanding from your precepts;
therefore I hate every wrong path.
Psalm 119:104

"Teenagers! I just don't know what to do with them." Have you ever felt that way or even said something like that out loud?

Parenting isn't easy and just when you think you've got a handle on one stage, your children move on to the next one. You can read every self-help book written and still just end up frustrated. The best thing to read and absorb is God's Word. Base your parenting skills on His guidelines for how to treat one another with love and respect.

While you may still want advice from other parents who have been through similar experiences, knowing God's guidelines for love, respect, patience, kindness, and discipline, and following them with consistency will help you be the best parent possible.

Speaking in Love

Speaking the truth in love, we will in all things grow up into him who is the Head, that is, Christ.
Ephesians 4:15

Do you know anyone who is so blunt that she hurts others' feelings and discourages the very people she thinks she is helping? If so, you probably notice that people try to avoid her – bluntness, even if it's the truth, is not generally appreciated.

That is a good thing for parents to remember. Sometimes, parents are so eager to share their opinions and values with their children that they just blurt it out and no love is apparent. More than likely their childrens' self-esteem will take a tumble from that kind of exchange.

It's important to share the truth of proper behavior, good choices, and high morals, but be careful to speak the truth in love. Your children will be more likely to listen to what you have to say.

Biting Your Tongue

When words are many, sin is not absent,
but he who holds his tongue is wise.
Proverbs 10:19

Constantly harping on your children, criticizing and correcting everything they do, offering your unsolicited opinion on every outfit they put on, questioning every decision they make, interrogating on a daily basis, will often cause you to lose ground with them rather than have the desired effect of maturing them. As difficult as it is, we have to let our children make some mistakes, even though we see them coming. Those fledgling efforts at making choices are the way they learn what works and what doesn't. Sometimes it's best for Mom and Dad to bite their tongues if the situation doesn't pose real danger for the child, and let their little sweetheart make a mistake ... and learn from it.

A Heritage

These are the commands, decrees and laws the LORD your God directed me to teach you to observe ... so that you, your children and their children after them may fear the LORD your God as long as you live by keeping all his decrees and commands that I give you.

Deuteronomy 6:1-2

You have the opportunity to start a lineage of faith, if it hasn't already begun in your family. The opportunity to pass down the truths and joys of the Christian life is a responsibility that should not be taken lightly.

If your children see that your faith "works", then they will be much more likely to make faith in God a way of life themselves. As they see the truth of the gospel incorporated into your life, they will learn to do the same and then some day in the future, pass that same lifestyle along to their children.

Good Training

*Train up a child in the way he should go,
and when he is old he will not turn from it.*
Proverbs 22:6

At one time or another most parents feel as if they have "blown it." You know your own shortcomings and you probably tend to focus on those and magnify them in relation to your parenting skills. If, as your children grow up, they make poor choices, your opinions of your failures grow. How can you be sure you are being a good parent?

The bottom line is that if you teach your children about God and the importance of loving and obeying Him and you truly love your child – that's the best you can do.

Trust God to remind them of the truths you have taught them. Realize that you have done your best and remember, at some point your children are responsible for their own choices.

Never Cease Praying

Pray continually.
1 Thessalonians 5:16

One of the most important things a mother can do for her children is pray for them. Pray for them every day. Lift them up to God asking Him to surround them with His protection. Ask Him to guide them in their choice of friends and activities. Ask Him to give them strength to stand firm in the choices they make.

Pray for their future decisions such as which college to attend and what career to follow. Pray for your child's future spouse. Ask God to direct that person's choices in life, too.

Surround your child with prayers for wisdom and strength. Pray for your own wisdom as you parent – each child is different and requires a different parenting approach. God will show you how to relate to each child and how to show your love to them.

Stay Close

*Pursue righteousness, godliness,
faith, love, endurance and gentleness.*
1 Timothy 6:11

Parenting is a full-time job and you are probably busier than you ever thought possible. As busy as you are, this is no time to let your devotional time and prayer time slide away. It's more important than ever that you pursue a lifestyle of staying close to the Lord and depending on Him for whatever life may bring.

The very fact that life is so busy demands that this be a priority because you need God's guidance and help in parenting. On a daily basis you will find that you need His help in consistently disciplining and guiding your children in love. You will need His help in being gentle and patient. Stay close to Him and pursue the process of becoming the kind of person He wants you to be.

Discipline is Good

Do not withhold discipline from a child; if you punish him with the rod, he will not die. Punish him with the rod and save his soul from death.

Proverbs 23:13-14

Have you ever seen a poorly behaved child throwing a temper tantrum? Or observed a child who doesn't play well with his peers? What were your thoughts about this child? "He needs a firm hand of discipline." Or, "Someone needs to teach him how to behave." If you thought such things, you are absolutely right.

Some parents don't like to discipline their children because they don't want their child to be angry with them or they want the child to experience freedom. Scriptures tell us that discipline is a good thing – it doesn't hurt your child. In fact, in the long run it will help him have more friends and a happier life.

Love Always

Do everything in love.
1 Corinthians 16:14

Love should motivate everything we do, especially as parents. That isn't always easy ... sometimes tiredness motivates us, or busyness or selfishness. Making love the filter through which all our actions are measured will keep our motives pure.

Loving our children means wanting the best for them. That means it is necessary to discipline them as well as hug them. Doing everything in love assures that you are helping your children become the people God wants them to be. Doing everything in love means that your children see you relating to your parents, boss, neighbors, Christian brothers and sisters in love. They will learn to do everything in love by watching you live that way.

Hard Work

If a man will not work, he shall not eat.
2 Thessalonians 3:10

Teach your children the joy of hard work. Let them work side by side with you doing yard work and housework. Teach them the proper way to do chores and allow the freedom for them to do their best – without you coming along behind and redoing the work to your own standards.

Let your children experience the joy of a completed job. Instill good work ethics in your children. You will be doing them a great service by giving them chores around the house for which they are responsible. They will learn to be accountable for jobs they are supposed to do.

These habits, instilled early on, will aid them when they get their first part-time job and even into adulthood as they begin their careers.

Controlled Temper

A hot-tempered man stirs up dissension,
but a patient man calms a quarrel.
Proverbs 15:18

It's very stressful to be around a person who explodes in anger for no obvious reason. You find yourself walking on eggshells around a person like this because you have no idea what will set off her temper. Not much fun to be around.

But think about this – are you a hot-tempered parent? Do you explode in anger when your children disobey or frustrate you? Do you see fear in their eyes?

It's difficult to respect a person who has a hot temper and that's as true of parents as it is of anyone. If you have temper problems, ask God to help you get it under control and help you to respond calmly and firmly but never in anger.

Good Marriage

Wives, submit to your husbands, as is fitting in the Lord. Husbands, love your wives and do not be harsh with them.

Colossians 3:18-19

You've heard it said before ... the best gift you can give your child is to love your spouse. Create a home life that is peaceful and pleasant. Give your children an assurance that their parents love each other and there is no danger of a divorce.

Let them see the proper way to resolve differences of opinion. Show respect for each other and model a proper way to treat your spouse. Work as a team with your spouse and show the strength of a husband and wife who stand together before God and who seek to help each other be the best people they can be.

Obedient Love

This is love: that we walk in obedience to his commands. As you have heard from the beginning, his command is that you walk in love.
2 John 6

Loving is obeying. Interesting lesson to teach your children. They show their love for you by obeying you to the best of their abilities. You show your love for God by obeying Him. You can assure your children that even grown-ups need to obey. Of course, you can tell your children that everyone disobeys sometimes ... even grown-ups ... but the goal is to obey more and more and more.

One of God's most important commands for us to obey is to love one another. So, that's a good starting point to remember. Love one another and obey God's commands.

A Happy Home

A happy heart makes the face
cheerful, but heartache crushes the spirit.
Proverbs 15:13

A family sat together in a restaurant, celebrating a birthday. Their conversation was heavily sprinkled with laughter. Conversation was animated and lighthearted, filled with happy memories. When the family got up to leave, another patron stopped them and commented that it was so nice to see a family enjoying each other so much.

Is your home a happy place? When you sit around the dinner table does conversation flow? Do your children enjoy sharing memories? Developing an atmosphere of love and trust in your home will instill a happy heart in each family member and that will make happy lives that will show the world that you enjoy being together.

Good Wisdom

*The wisdom that comes from heaven
is first of all pure; then peace-loving,
considerate, submissive, full of mercy
and good fruit, impartial and sincere.*
James 3:17

Living in God's wisdom fills your life with good qualities that make you pleasant to be around, a good spouse, good parent and good friend. Seeking to live by God's wisdom helps you to be considerate of other people, especially the people you live with, which is sometimes the hardest.

It will help you be submissive to others, seeking to lift them up and please them instead of yourself. You will be kind and compassionate to others' needs. Your love will be sincere and fair. These are wonderful qualities to live out before your children, and to instill in them.

Cheerleaders!

*Let us consider how we may spur one
another on toward love and good deeds.*
Hebrews 10:24

The joy of living in a family is that family members can encourage one another to try new things and explore their talents and gifts. They can be cheerleaders for each other! When a child hits the game-winning homerun, spells a word right in the spelling bee or sings a solo in church, she looks at her parents to see if they're proud of her.

Take every opportunity to reinforce your child's good behaviors. Help your child develop sensitivity to other people. Involve your child in efforts to help others, whether at Christmas time or year round by working in a homeless shelter or food pantry. Teach your child the joy of serving others and help her find ways she can do so.

MARCH

Friendship

Drop It

Starting a quarrel is like breaching a dam;
so drop the matter before a dispute breaks out.
Proverbs 17:14

Friends are wonderful, especially when you have similar opinions and values. When friends agree with everything you think, conversation is easy.

But what happens when a friend disagrees with you and firmly expresses her opinion? Do you find yourself quarreling with friends, causing rifts in your friendships? Is your opinion so important to you that it is worth these possibly damaging breaks in your friendships?

When you see a quarrel coming, do you stand your ground and ready yourself for the fight? Here's a different approach ... drop it. Value the friendship more than your opinion. Show your friend how important she is to you.

Going Out of Your Way

*"He ... bandaged his wounds ... Then he put the
man on his own donkey, took him to an inn
and took care of him. The next day he took out
two silver coins and gave them to the innkeeper."*
Luke 10:34-35

What's the best way to help a friend with a problem?
Pray for her, then go on your way? Prayer is
certainly important. But the lesson learned from
this passage shows us that if we go out of our way
to help someone – even inconvenience ourselves,
or spend our time and money – we will be showing
true friendship.

So, always and energetically pray for your friends.
But, if you have the material means to tangibly meet
some of their needs ... do that, too. It shows real,
true and active friendship in a way that nothing
else can.

Sharing with Others

Do not forget to do good and to share with others for with such sacrifices God is pleased.
Hebrews 13:16

It is impossible to be a friend if you are unwilling to share. Being a friend means caring about someone and desiring to help them and meet their needs in any way you can. This means sharing your time, your possessions and your heart.

When your friend needs your help or your listening ear, you must share your time, even if it isn't really a convenient time for you. Friendship doesn't always happen on your time schedule. True friendship requires the sacrifice of putting your own preferences and desires aside and being there for your friend when she needs you. You would want your friend to be willing to do that for you, wouldn't you?

Support System

*Two are better than one, because they have
a good return for their work: If one falls down,
his friend can help him up. But pity the man
who falls and has no one to help him up!*
Ecclesiastes 4:9-10

Accountability with help attached. One of the benefits and responsibilities of friendship is that when you stumble and fall, your friend helps you up.

What does this mean in practical terms? Let's say you're being loudly critical of another person. A good friend (who has earned your trust) could gently point this out and help you control or even change your attitude. The power of two can make love stronger and help each of you live out God's purpose in this world. But if you are alone, by situation or by choice, it's much harder to be strong or even to know when you need to change something in your life.

Marks of Friendship

*Therefore, as God's chosen people, holy and
dearly loved, clothe yourselves with compassion,
kindness, humility, gentleness and patience.*

Colossians 3:12

This verse about covers it, doesn't it? These are the qualities you would want in a friend – compassion to share your pain, kindness to help you through hard times and to celebrate good ones, humility that lets you sometimes win and that lifts you up, gentleness when you disappoint and patience to let you try again.

If you have a friend with these qualities, thank God for her. But remember the command in this equation – you are to clothe yourself with these qualities, so you will bring these same qualities to your friendships. Remember, too, that you don't get to choose some of these qualities and ignore the others. They are each to become a part of your personality ... and to be shared with your friends.

A Learning Process

As iron sharpens iron, so
one man sharpens another.
Proverbs 27:17

Believe it or not, you don't know everything about everything ... and neither do your friends. There will always be more to learn on a topic and more to understand about other people and situations in our world.

Friendship is important to that process. Through stimulating discussions, differing view-points and challenging observations, you will learn and grow. Appreciate what your friends can do for you in this area – and you for them. Make time to engage in conversations about various topics and see what you can learn. Give your friends the freedom to honestly share their opinions, even if they are different from yours. You might be surprised at how your attitude can change when you really listen and understand another's viewpoint.

Gentle Friends

Let your gentleness be evident to all.
Philippians 4:5

What do you think of when you hear the word "gentleness"? Perhaps it means a quiet and kind attitude, or a soft and loving tone of voice. It might mean that someone has patience with you when you make friendship mistakes.

Gentleness can mean seeing your friend quietly put her own agenda aside and willingly assist you with things in your life. Gentleness is a reflection of the way Jesus related to people He came in contact with. Living a life of gentleness shows Christ's love to others.

If you have a gentle friend, thank God for her and in that prayer of thanks, ask God to help you to also be that kind of friend.

Forgiving Friendship

*Be kind and compassionate to
one another, forgiving each other,
just as in Christ God forgave you.*
Ephesians 4:32

One of the marks of true friendship is forgiveness – with no strings attached. We all make mistakes, inadvertently hurting or disappointing our friends. Most of the time hurting doesn't happen on purpose. Isn't it an amazing relief when your friend forgives you for hurtful mistakes?

The fact is that when each of us steps back from life for a minute and thinks about how much God forgives us ... daily ... the little bit of forgiving we might do for our friends amounts to a hill of beans. So, willingly forgive your friends. Be an example of God's loving forgiveness to others.

Kind Words

*A word aptly spoken is like apples
of gold in settings of silver.*
Proverbs 25:11

The power of words is amazing! How many times have carelessly spoken words (or deliberately delivered cruel words) stabbed your heart? Unkind words can pierce our very self-esteem, making joy, hope and love leak from our hearts.

But kind, encouraging words spoken in love may lift us from despair, put hope in our hearts and a bounce in our steps. What about you ... can your friends count on hopeful, encouraging words from you? Or do your friends expect sarcastic and generally unkind comments from you? If it's the latter, why not make a change? Make a point of making your words beautiful and kind so that they are a pleasure to all who receive them.

No Fakes!

Love must be sincere.
Romans 12:9

You see her walk into church, school or the coffee shop and you want to run. She's always so sweet and gushy that you can almost feel your blood sugar level rising. This woman so overdoes the appearances of concern and love for you that you know, without a doubt, that it's an act. She doesn't mean a word of it. Consequently, you don't believe she truly cares a bit about you.

What's missing? Sincerity. For all her efforts at showing love to you, it just doesn't sell. It's all surface. Love must be sincere if it is going to be believable. So, if you don't really love someone, you can still be kind and respectful, but don't bother gushing. Instead, ask God to grow love for that person in your heart. Be open to His work and see what happens!

Listen Up

The way of a fool seems right to him,
but a wise man listens to advice.
Proverbs 12:15

To whom do you go for advice? Perhaps parents or siblings ... or a good friend? If you are blessed with a truly good friend, one whom you trust and respect, one who waits to be asked her opinion and advice, rather than dumping it on you, then listen to that friend.

When you have a decision to make or a problem to handle, take time to sit down together and talk things through. Show how wise you are by hearing what your friend has to say. Another set of eyes and a different viewpoint can help you see a more complete picture than you see on your own. A wise friend is a true gift from God.

Proper Procedures

"If your brother sins against you, go and show him his fault, just between the two of you. If he listens to you, you have won your brother over."
Matthew 18:15

How do you handle a problem with a friend? Do you deal with it privately or publicly?

According to this verse, the proper thing to do is to go to your friend and discuss the problem ... just the two of you. That means you don't complain about your friend to others. You shouldn't tear down her reputation by telling your side of the story to other friends, especially when she isn't there to defend herself. The least amount of damage will be done to the relationship if you handle problems privately. If that doesn't work, the next verses in Matthew 18 tell you what to do next.

Follow the proper procedures and save the friendship.

Unity

*How good and pleasant it is when
brothers live together in unity!*

Psalm 133:1

Oneness. Single-minded purpose and action. This is true friendship that glorifies God and is an example of His love to all who observe it. Real friendship is a gift from God and is to be treasured. Friends encourage us through difficult times and celebrate with us in good times.

We tend to gravitate toward people who are much like we are in their values and goals. So, living and working together in unity is very important as we seek to help each other become the people that God intends. When a friendship hits a speed bump, it is important to deal with it immediately, then continue moving forward in unity so that each person can continue growing and the friendship will continue showing Christlike unity to all who observe it.

Spirit-Filled Living

*Let us not become conceited,
provoking and envying each other.*
Galatians 5:26

This verse immediately follows the verses where Paul described the fruit of the Spirit. He pointed out that those who are filled with the Spirit make every effort to keep in step with the Spirit. Isn't it interesting that Paul closed this section with this call to humbleness?

It is practically impossible to get along with others when you are full of yourself. Every time you raise yourself above others, you push them down. That kind of treatment can really upset others and cause people to avoid spending time with you. Examine your own behavior – are you living a Spirit-filled life? Are others blessed by your presence in their lives or do your actions provoke bad behavior in them? Decide to be a blessing to others.

Helping Each Other

"The man with two tunics should share
with him who has none, and the
one who has food should do the same."
Luke 3:11

Our world today is focused on more ... getting a better job, bigger house, fancier car, more stuff, more stuff, more stuff. The more "stuff" you have the more successful you are perceived to be. In fact, some people make it a personal challenge to acquire more stuff than anyone else.

The more godly way to live is pretty much the opposite of the "stuff-getting" mentality. It is to share. When people around you have needs and you have the material means to meet those needs ... do it. It's fine to pray for people with needs, that's certainly important. But go the extra step and help people when you can ... share what you have.

False Claims

Anyone who claims to be in the light
but hates his brother is still in the darkness.
1 John 2:9

This verse shows a tight link between relationships and living in the Spirit. The truth is, you can speak all the Christianeze you know ... you can work day and night at the church ... you can give until your wallet is empty; but if you don't love your brothers and sisters, you are walking in darkness. You can think you're fooling people ... maybe you are ... but you're not fooling God.

So, if you have schisms in your relationships, sit down and talk it out. Settle your differences and get over the negative feelings. Then you can begin walking in the light and serving God with a pure heart.

True Friendship

A friend loves at all times.
Proverbs 17:17

No matter what happens, a true friend is true. More than likely, sometimes your friend will mess up. Once in a while your friend may disappoint you or even hurt you. What will your response be? Well, sometimes you may lose your cool and get angry with your friend. Sometimes you may just need some space from her ... but after the initial response, what's next? Can you get past your feelings and love your friend no matter what?

A friend is able to get past the emotions that may be self-centered, and past the unintentional hurt. A true friend loves all the time. That means giving your friend the benefit of the doubt and looking for the good, no matter what. Love your friend in the same way you want her to love you.

Friends Helping Friends

We who are strong ought to bear with the failings of the weak and not to please ourselves. Each of us should please his neighbor for his good, to build him up.
Romans 15:1-2

God created us as relational people. We need one another, we find joy and comfort in those we love. Our relationships are examples of God Himself, who, as the Father, Son and Holy Spirit is a community.

Your friends can keep you accountable in your Christian walk, they can encourage you to grow and stretch and become the person God wants you to be. You can do the same for them. Friends look for unselfish ways to help friends grow and learn. God put friends in your life for a reason and He put you in your friends' lives for a reason. Be the best friend you can be.

A Second Look

*Jonathan took off the robe he was wearing
and gave it to David, along with his tunic,
and even his sword, his bow and his belt.*

1 Samuel 18:4

Jonathan and David had an interesting relationship. Jonathan was in line to be the next king, but David was God's choice to lead His people. Jonathan's father did not like David, so the likelihood of Jonathan and David becoming friends was not great. But they did. They saw through situations, past other's opinions, and looked at each other's heart and found true, lasting friendship.

Are there potential friends in your world – someone whom you haven't given a chance, for one reason or another? Give that person another chance. You just may find a golden friendship; a Jonathan and David friendship.

Honesty Time

*"Therefore, if you are offering your gift at the altar
and there remember that your brother has
something against you, leave your gift there
in front of the altar. First go and be reconciled
to your brother; then come and offer your gift."*

Matthew 5:23-24

Let's assume you know all the right things to say,
the verses to quote, the things to do ... you've got
Christianity down pat. But, when it comes to handling relationship problems ... well, you've got a few
things to learn. One important lesson is outlined
in this verse – don't pretend!

You might be able to fool the people around you
into thinking that your Christian walk is flawless,
but God knows when you've got unresolved problems with friends and so do those friends. Get
those things straightened out, then get
on with your Christian walk.

Watch Your Words

Do not let any unwholesome talk come out
of your mouths, but only what is helpful
for building others up according to their
needs, that it may benefit those who listen.
Ephesians 4:29

So many verses in Scripture are devoted to watching our speech that we know it must truly be a problem. Unwholesome talk can take many forms. It's fun to make people laugh, but is your humor at the expense of a friend?

What about gossip? Even "innocent news" shared with a friend about another friend may be unwholesome talk. The bottom line is everything you say about a friend should build up that person; encourage her; make her look good to others. Your friends should be able to count on you for kind and encouraging words.

The Evidence of God

*No one has ever seen God; but if we
love one another, God lives in us
and his love is made complete in us.*

1 John 4:12

Wow, there's quite a responsibility outlined in this verse. Did you see it? No one has ever seen God, but the way we relate to one another, the love we show, is the way God is seen in the world. Whew! That cuts through the garbage we often encase our relationships in, doesn't it? No pretending, no shallowness, no self-serving ego, no righteous in-dignation ... nothing but love.

The evidence of God living in you is that you truly, honestly love the people around you. The wonderful thing is that you can enjoy your friends, love them, celebrate them, appreciate them, and be evidence of God's presence in this world at the same time.

Choose Good Friends

A righteous man is cautious in friendship,
but the way of the wicked leads them astray.
Proverbs 12:26

You don't get to choose your family. You're born into a family and there they are, with all their little quirks and oddities. But you do get to choose your friends.

Be careful about the people you choose to spend time with. Make sure that your friends share your values and that their influence in your life will be positive.

Friends can stretch you and challenge you to grow but they shouldn't pull you away from your faith. They shouldn't lead you down a path that leads to dishonesty either.

Think carefully through your choice of friends. Choose friends who will encourage you and help you to glorify God.

Working Together

The body is a unit, though it is made up of many parts; and though all its parts are many, they form one body.
1 Corinthians 12:12

Friends are important because they complete you. God put you on this earth and equipped you to do a job. Your work for God will be easier and more effective if you work side by side with other people. The friends you choose can help you learn what your spiritual gifts are and can help you understand how to put them into practice.

This verse reinforces the fact that we are better off with friends around us, rather than trying to go through life alone. Just as your physical body has individual parts, but is only complete and healthy when all those parts work together, so your life is more complete with friends who work beside you, lift you up, challenge you ... and love you.

Judge Not

"Do not judge, or you too will be judged.
For in the same way you judge others,
you will be judged, and with the
measure you use, it will be measured to you."

Matthew 7:1-2

Know anyone who is quick to point out your flaws but never seems to have any flaws herself? Perhaps this "friend" thinks she is doing you a favor by pointing out areas of your character that you need to work on, but more than likely all she succeeds in doing is making you want to avoid her.

Well, how do you relate to others? Are you quick to judge? Jesus said that we will be judged by the same standard we use for others. Have you attained some level of perfection that qualifies you to judge another person? Not likely. Be careful to cut others the same amount of slack with which you yourself wish to be judged.

Sacrificial Living

*Dear children, let us not love with words
or tongue but with actions and in truth.*
1 John 3:18

Love is defined by action. You can say loving things. You can promise to pray. But what action can your love take? In this busy, hectic world what does it mean to actively love?

It involves setting priorities and making time for the important things rather than letting urgent things take up your time. It means making a meal for a friend who is overwhelmed with mommyhood. It means taking her children for an afternoon so she can have a few hours of respite. It means speaking up in support of her when someone else is tearing her down. Laying down your life for your friend means giving whatever you can to meet whatever needs she has anytime you can.

Loving Others

Love your neighbor as yourself. Love does no harm to its neighbor. Therefore love is the fulfillment of the law.
Romans 13:9-10

Perhaps you read this verse and think, "I don't love myself. I see all my shortcomings and failings. I'm not happy with me." Well, think about it. You probably look out for Number One pretty consistently – make sure you have food, clothing, a warm place to sleep and that your basic needs are met. You probably get sufficiently irritated if you feel you've been slighted in any way. The point is you do love yourself enough to look out for yourself.

Do you love others in the same way? Love looks for ways to encourage and help. It never seeks to do harm to others. Love is the way God wants us to live together.

Winning with Kindness

A kindhearted woman gains respect,
but ruthless men gain only wealth.
Proverbs 11:16

Think about the people in your life whom you respect. Do they have anything in common? More than likely they are kind people who treat others well. Is kindness a trait you value in your own life? If you make a point to consistently treat those around you with kindness, they will know they have value to you. Your kind words will build them up so that they believe in themselves and they can achieve more and more in life.

Being treated kindly is vital to good self-esteem, which is vital to growth of skills and talents, which is vital to serving God. Just as you respect those who are kind to you, others will respect you for kindnesses shown.

Growing Pains

Make every effort to add to your faith goodness;
and to goodness, knowledge; and to knowledge,
self-control; and to self-control, perseverance; and
to perseverance, godliness; and to godliness,
brotherly kindness; and to brotherly kindness, love.

2 Peter 1:5-7

Look at the process outlined in these verses. It begins with faith and moves to love. Along the continuum, you pick up knowledge, self-control, perseverance, godliness and kindness.

Think about how valuable these characteristics are in friendship. They build on one another. You won't be loving if you aren't first kind, which comes easier to one who is godly. Godliness is learned through perseverance, which begins with self-control, which is based on knowledge, which is motivated by goodness.

What an awesome group of values and character traits to bring to friendship.

Turn the Other Cheek

"You have heard that it was said, 'Eye for eye and tooth for tooth.' But, I tell you, do not resist an evil person. If someone strikes you on the right cheek, turn to him the other also."

Matthew 5:38-39

Friendship is wonderful when everything is going well and you're getting along with your friends. But what about when you hit a speed bump? When your friend hurts you, intentionally or not, how do you respond? Do you live by the "eye for an eye" philosophy and seek to get even with your friend? If so, you probably do so as secretly as possible. After all, you don't want to look like the bad guy, you just want justice, right?

Well, God's justice is different from yours. He says to forget the whole getting even thing and turn the other cheek. Just let it go and live in love.

Rows of Dominoes

*Let us consider how we may spur one
another on toward love and good deeds.*
Hebrews 10:24

Friendship should bring out the best in you and your friends. Your friendship can encourage others and actually make them better people. Think about it … the confidence that someone cares for you, believes in you, serves you and sacrifices for you encourages you to do the same for those around you.

One act of kindness becomes the impetus for a row of falling dominoes, tumbling one good deed into another. Spurring one another toward love and good deeds will show the world the power of love – God's love growing in your heart and being shared with others. It will make the world a better place.

APRIL

Shine His Light

Outside the Church

> *They asked his disciples, "Why does your*
> *teacher eat with tax collectors and sinners?"*
> *On hearing this, Jesus said, "It is not the*
> *healthy who need a doctor, but the sick."*
> Matthew 9:11-12

The church isn't just here for Christians. Jesus' statement reminds us that we shouldn't get comfortably settled in our pews and let the world go by.

Jesus went out to where the people were who needed to know that God loved them. He spent time with the "undesirables" of His day. We must be careful not to get comfortable in our church where we all look the same, believe the same, and have the same social standards. We must remember that there is a whole world full of people who don't yet know about God's love. It's up to us to tell them.

Patient Fisherman

"Come, follow me," Jesus said,
"and I will make you fishers of men."
Matthew 4:19

Fishing takes patience. You can sit in the boat or on the dock for hours at a time before you actually catch a fish; in fact sometimes you don't catch one at all. But usually patience and diligence pay off. So, it's interesting that Jesus used fishing to describe the process of winning people to Him. He promises to make us fishermen.

God has given each of us unique gifts and talents and Jesus uses those to make each of us fishermen. We work within our strengths. He doesn't ask us to do things He has not given us the ability to do. It takes patience and diligence, but the reward is seeing souls come to Him!

Team Colors

*Never be lacking in zeal, but keep
your spiritual fervor, serving the Lord.*
Romans 12:11

Turn on the television any Sunday afternoon in November or December and you will observe thousands of people with zeal! They cheer for their favorite football team, dress in the team colors, wear silly hats, and perhaps even paint their faces in the team colors. They are passionate about their team.

Can you imagine Christians with crosses painted on their faces, wearing team shirts, shouting out praises to Jesus? Can you see them going into the neighborhood and spreading their enthusiasm for the Lord?

Paul encouraged us to keep our zeal and our fervor – our joy in serving the Lord. It's the excitement and joy that will draw others to want to know Christ.

A Position of Honor

We are therefore Christ's ambassadors,
as though God were making his appeal
through us. We implore you on Christ's
behalf: Be reconciled to God.
2 Corinthians 5:20

An ambassador represents his home country in a foreign land. He speaks for his government and attends official functions on the President's behalf. It is a position of authority and honor.

We are Christ's ambassadors; His representatives in this world. He desires to speak through us, sharing the gospel message of hope and salvation with the world. We must make ourselves available to Him. The almighty God can certainly accomplish His purposes without us. But we have been given a position of honor and responsibility to be available for God to use us to encourage people to be reconciled to Him.

Be Ready

*Do your best to present yourself to
God as one approved, a workman
who does not need to be ashamed and
who correctly handles the word of truth.*
2 Timothy 2:15

Do not take your position as God's workman lightly. It comes with a responsibility. If God has given you the privilege of sharing the truths of His Word with others, be sure you are doing it correctly. As you mark out a path for others to walk down on their journey to knowing Jesus, be careful to study God's Word and correctly present it.

This verse isn't meant to scare you away from witnessing, only to take the privilege of sharing God's message seriously and to always be prepared.

A Good Defense

In your hearts set apart Christ as Lord.
Always be prepared to give an answer
to everyone who asks you to give
the reason for the hope that you have.
1 Peter 3:15

The best defense is a good offense. We live in a sophisticated world where education and intelligence are highly valued. In order to share the message of salvation with people, you must be ready to share and you must know what you're talking about.

Take advantage of learning opportunities in your church in order to have a clearer understanding of the Bible and be able to articulately defend your faith. Hopefully, you will also have practical life examples of how God interacts in the world. Knowledge and experience are two key ingredients for giving the reason for the hope that you have.

Come Forward, Workers

*"The harvest is plentiful but the workers
are few. Ask the Lord of the harvest, therefore
to send out workers into his harvest field."*
Matthew 9:37-38

God, in His infinite wisdom, decided to allow us, His children, to participate in the process of bringing other people to Him. It's a privilege we take all too lightly.

Jesus knew that there were plenty of people who needed to hear the gospel message and, in fact, were waiting to hear it. But the workers were not coming forward. He asked His disciples to pray for workers to come forward.

We must do the same ... pray for workers who are willing to leave their homes, and possibly their homelands, to share the message of God's love with all who will listen.

Growing Believers

*I planted the seed, Apollos
watered it, but God made it grow.*
1 Corinthians 3:6

God gives each of us gifts and talents. Some of us are seed planters, making an initial contact with a person, perhaps giving them their first contact with a Christian. Another person is the one who waters. This person has a longer contact with the unbeliever, gently watering the seed that was planted, waiting for the water to settle, then watering again.

Each of us must do our job and we must work as a team for a seed to be planted. However, it is not any of our responsibility to make the seed grow – only God can do that. If we each do our jobs, He will do the rest.

Be Ready

*Preach the Word; be prepared in season
and out of season; correct, rebuke and encourage –
with great patience and careful instruction.*
2 Timothy 4:2

Do you read this verse and think, "But, I'm no minister!" You don't have to be. But, as a believer, you do need to read God's Word and learn how it applies to your life. What you learn are lessons that can be shared in everyday conversation and friendship.

Know the Word, be ready to share it – when it's easy and when it isn't. Gently use God's Word to show the right way to live and the right choices to make. Be careful to be patient with those you share with. Be careful to correctly give instructions from the Word. Be careful, but be firm.

Don't Be Lazy

*A curse on him who is lax
in doing the LORD's work!*
Jeremiah 48:10

Whoa! This is serious. God does not kid around about His work. He doesn't save us so that we can sit down in a padded pew, hold a hymnal in front of our faces and take a nap. There is work to do and God wants us to do it. God does not want anyone in the entire world to die without having had the opportunity to hear about Him and His love.

How will people hear if we don't tell them? Don't be lazy. Don't be afraid. Just get up and get busy doing the job God has given you for this day. Do the Lord's work.

Get Busy!

"As long as it is day, we must do the work of him who sent me. Night is coming, when no one can work."
John 9:4

Jesus spoke these words to encourage His followers to get busy. There is work to be done and that work is to win others to God.

Jesus Himself was busy with that work the whole time He walked this earth. He warns that a time is coming when it will be too late to share the gospel. No one will be able to respond to it in that day.

Do you sense the urgency? Get up, get busy and do the work God gave you to do while there is still time. When night comes ... when the time for deciding is over ... it's too late.

Practical Advice

Carry each other's burdens, and in this
way you will fulfill the law of Christ.
Galatians 6:2

Christ taught that the greatest commandment is to love God with all your heart, soul, and mind and the second is to love your neighbor as yourself. When another person is hurting and you have the ability or wherewithal to help that person ... do it. That may be the most effective witness you can give.

You can stand in front of a hurting person and preach about God's love ... but putting your message into action and actually helping her will probably go a lot farther than just your words would.

Share Christ's love in real ways, then add the words to your action for a complete message.

A "How-To"

*Your word is a lamp to my
feet and a light for my path.*
Psalm 119:105

"I want to witness for God, but I just don't know what to do or say!" Here's the antidote for those feelings: Let God guide your steps and your words. Ask Him to direct you to someone who needs to know about Him. Ask Him to give you the correct words to say.

Spend time in His Word so you know it and can share from it the truth that every person is a sinner, Christ died for our sins and rose again. Know His Word so you can share the plan of salvation from it. Be able to share examples of how God has guided your footsteps through His Word.

Party On!

*"If he finds it, I tell you the truth, he is happier
about that one sheep than about the ninety-nine
that did not wander off. In the same way
your Father in heaven is not willing that
any of these little ones should be lost."*
Matthew 18:13-14

Jesus had just shared the parable of the lost sheep
with His disciples. This parable recounts how
a shepherd had 100 sheep and one got lost. He
left the ninety-nine to go and find that one lost
sheep. When he found it, he celebrated with joy.

Jesus said that God feels that way about people.
He doesn't want anyone to be lost for eternity – not
even one person. That means that He wants all
people to have the opportunity to choose to accept
the gospel message.

If the whole world is going to hear the gospel,
we'd better get busy!

The Best Gift

*Praise be to the Lord, for he
showed his wonderful love to me.*
Psalm 31:21

What is the most wonderful gift you have ever been given? Think about it for a minute. What made it so special? Who gave it to you? After you received it, what did you do? Did you tell anyone? Did you celebrate?

The most wonderful gift imaginable is the truth that God loves you. He loves you unconditionally, completely, and eternally. What kind of response does that evoke in your heart? Are you going to keep quiet about His love? Do you feel like celebrating? How about sharing? It's certainly not something you can keep quiet about, right? Then tell someone today about His wonderful love. Tell how you are aware of His love in your daily life.

Witness!

*You will receive power when the Holy
Spirit comes on you; and you will be
my witnesses in Jerusalem, and in all Judea
and Samaria, and to the ends of the earth.*

Acts 1:8

A couple of important observations from this verse:
One, Jesus doesn't say, "You might be my witnesses … or some of you will be my witnesses." He says
you *will* be my witnesses.

The second thing is that we don't have to be
a witness in our own strength. He sent the Holy
Spirit to help us do this work. The bottom line is
that we're all witnesses for something – whatever is
most important to us in life. Are you witnessing for
Jesus or for something like well-decorated houses.
Make sure your witness is for Jesus, then ask Him
where He wants you to do the witnessing.

Great Commission

*"Therefore, go and make disciples of all
nations, baptizing them in the name
of the Father and of the Son and of the Holy
Spirit and teaching them to obey everything
I have commanded you. And surely, I am
with you always, to the very end of the age."*
Matthew 28:19-20

Through the years this passage has come to be
known as The Great Commission and it is often used
at mission conferences to try to motivate people to
take up missionary service. It certainly leaves no
doubt as to what is important to Jesus.

The command is plain – He wants all nations to
know Him and follow Him. He wants all nations to
be taught to obey God. These verses leave no doubt
as to how we should be spending our time. The
assurance at the end is wonderful – He is with us.
We never have to feel that we're working alone.

Healthy Bodies

*Each of us has one body with many members,
and these members do not all have the same
function, so in Christ we who are many form one
body, and each member belongs to all the others.*
Romans 12:14

A healthy body has many, many functioning parts. Some are visible to the observing eye and some are not. But each part is important to the ongoing health of the body and its proper functioning.

So it is with the local church body. God places different people with different gifts in each body. Each person must do their job or the body will not be healthy. In order for souls to be won to Christ, each of us must do our job. We're all on the same team, reaching for the same goal. So we must work together.

Active Love

*"I was hungry and you gave me something
to eat, I was thirsty and you gave me something
to drink, I was a stranger and you invited me in."*
Matthew 25:35

Jesus said that if we meet the physical needs of those around us, it is the same as meeting those needs for Him.

When you come across a person who does not have warm clothes or any food to eat, what do you do? Do you pat her on the back and say, "I'll pray for you," or do you find some way to give her food and clothing, then pray with her, thanking God for providing? What good is it to share words about God's love with someone who is too hungry or in too much pain to listen? Show God's love, then tell about it.

The Light

"You are the light of the world. A city on a hill cannot be hidden. Neither do people light a lamp and put it under a bowl ... in the same way, let your light shine before men, that they may see your good deeds and praise your Father in heaven."
Matthew 5:14-16

Have you ever been in such total darkness that you could not see your hand in front of your face? It's kind of a scary place to be. But when the tiniest glimmer of light comes in, it's such a good feeling. It seems to bring hope. That's the kind of responsibility you have, as Christ's ambassador in the world. Your life that shines with His love and values is a light in a dark world. Those who are burdened by life and who have no hope, will see the light and be drawn to it.

Instruction Manual

*All Scripture is God-breathed and is useful
for teaching, rebuking, correcting and
training in righteousness, so that the man of God
may be thoroughly equipped for every good work.*
2 Timothy 3:16-17

Every job is easier if you have an instruction manual. Programming the DVD player is a piece of cake … if you read the instructions.

God's work is easier, too, with the instruction manual He has provided. God's Word, the Bible, teaches us, corrects us, challenges us, and trains us to do any work He gives us to do. Even the privilege of sharing His love with others is made easier by knowing His Word. Don't go into your work ill-equipped. Know His Word and let God use it in your life.

Lighthouse

For this is what the Lord has commanded us:
"I have made you a light for the Gentiles, that
you may bring salvation to the ends of the earth."
Acts 13:47

The interesting thing about doing God's work on earth is that it will never be finished. As long as we are alive, God has a job for us to do. God doesn't want any people to miss the chance to know the joy of salvation. We have been entrusted with that message and it is both our privilege and our responsibility to share it.

God has made each of us a light. Our light, proclaiming His love, can shine like a lighthouse for those who are trying to find their way through the storms of life.

Patience

The Lord is not slow in keeping his promise,
as some understand slowness. He is patient
with you, not wanting anyone to perish,
but everyone to come to repentance.

2 Peter 3:9

Do you sometimes look at the mess our world is in and wonder why Christ doesn't just come back and end the horrific things? Why doesn't He put a stop to senseless wars, child abuse, murders and all the other things that make life so dangerous? He could. He could come at any moment. He's not slow in returning as some might think.

God, in His incredible love and patience, doesn't want anyone to miss out on salvation. All people have the freedom to choose Him or not. He's hoping that all say yes. But they can't say yes if they haven't heard. That's where we come in. We are to share the story of salvation every chance we get.

Eternal Security

*"My sheep listen to my voice; I know them,
and they follow me. I give them eternal
life, and they shall never perish;
no one can snatch them out of my hand."*
John 10:27-28

Eternal life. Never perish. These are two powerful phrases found in these verses. They are the reasons we should be sharing the gospel message every chance we get. Is the reality of eternity fixed in your mind? Do you believe there is a hell where people who do not know Christ will actually perish – with no reprieve?

When that reality looms in your mind, you will be moved to actively and eagerly tell people of God's love. Jesus promised that none of His sheep would perish. His sheep know His voice and follow Him. Following Him keeps us safe – forever.

Eager Sharing

*The woman went back to the town and said
to the people, "Come, see a man who told me
everything I did. Could this be the Christ?" ...
Many of the Samaritans from that town believed
in him because of the woman's testimony.*

John 4:28-29, 39

The woman at the well met Jesus quite unexpectedly.
She was an outcast in society, not the kind of person
you would expect to turn into an avid missionary.
But as she talked with Jesus and the reality of who
He was began to sink into her heart, she couldn't
keep quiet about Him. She raced back to town and
told everyone about Him.

She had found something in Him that she wanted
others to know about. She apparently shared without
inhibitions and because of her, many people came
to Christ that day. She is a good example for us.

Jesus' Work

*"The Son of Man came to seek
and save what was lost."*
Luke 19:10

Jesus knew His purpose. He had a reason to walk this earth. He was part of a plan to restore life to mankind; to give people the opportunity to know God and to share in His heaven. Every one of Jesus' actions, every word He spoke, was with this purpose in mind. In fact, He spoke these words because a sinful man named Zacchaeus had repented of his sin.

Jesus trained His disciples to carry on His work when He had gone back to heaven. We benefit from that training by reading the Bible and learning what Jesus taught. We are to continue the work of bringing the message of God's love to a lost world. Jesus doesn't want any people to perish.

The Message of Hope

*Jesus said to her, "I am the resurrection and
the life. He who believes in me will live,
even though he dies; and whoever
lives and believes in me will never die."*

John 11:25-26

Here is the heart of our message for the world. Jesus offers eternal life to those who believe in Him. He came to earth, died for our sins and was resurrected. Now we who believe in Him can live forever with Him in heaven.

This is the heart of the message we have to share with a lost world. It's the hope of our salvation. All people on earth will die eventually, everyone knows that, but there is no reason to die without hope. It is possible to know that heaven is sure and eternity can be spent there. Share the message, people are waiting to hear it.

Time Is Short

*"I tell you, open your eyes and look at the
fields! They are ripe for harvest. Even now
the reaper draws his wages, even now he
harvests the crop for eternal life so that the
sower and the reaper may be glad together."*

John 4:35-36

The fields are ready for harvest. God knows that
people, many people, are ready to hear the salvation
message. They are ready to accept Christ, but they
have to hear the message. It must make Him sad
that some of those He has appointed to sow the
seed are not doing the job.

Each of us has a role to play in bringing others
to Christ. You may sow, you may water, you may
reap. Whatever your job is, get busy and do it.
Time is short.

MAY

In Times of Discouragement

Working Out His Plan

*He who began a good work in you will carry
it on to completion until the day of Christ Jesus.*
Philippians 1:6

Are you experiencing a time when it seems like everything is going wrong and problems are piling one on top of the other? It's hard not to get discouraged during these times.

Paul reminds you that God has not forgotten you – even during the tough times of life. God's work in your life is not cursory. He doesn't get tired or busy with other things and forget about you. He has a plan for you and will continue working out that plan all of your life. So, in the depths of discouragement, try to remember that the things happening to you are not outside of God's knowledge. Lean on Him, call on Him and trust Him.

Support Base

*Cast all your anxiety on
him because he cares for you.*
1 Peter 5:7

Imagine a strength so powerful that you can pour all your fears, pain, problems, insecurities and anxieties into it and know they will be handled ... forever. That's God's love. He invites you to bring all of those things to Him and leave them at the foot of the cross. He will comfort you, strengthen you and encourage you because He cares about you. His care was shown in a very real way when Christ voluntarily came to earth to show, by example, how to live with others and for God.

He took your sin on Himself when He died on the cross and now He lives in heaven, making intercession for you. He knows what life on earth is like and He's willing to help you through it. Just ask Him.

Bodyguards

He will command his angels concerning you to guard you in all your ways; they will lift you up in their hands, so that you will not strike your foot against a stone.
Psalm 91:11-12

One of the worst things about discouragement is that you often feel as if no one truly understands what you're going through. Sometimes you may even sense that your family and friends are tired of hearing about your problems and are beginning to avoid you. You can end up feeling very alone in your struggles.

Well, you're not. Nothing that happens to you surprises God. He knows when you need extra strength and protection and He has appointed guardians to take care of His children. You may not even know what you have been protected from ... but rest assured that you are not alone.

Crossing Guard

*Even though I walk through the valley of the
shadow of death, I will fear no evil, for you are
with me; your rod and your staff, they comfort me.*

Psalm 23:4

If you've ever lost a loved one to death or faced death yourself, you may have found comfort in this verse.

Death can bring a fear of the unknown ... the crossing from this life to the next. We know, however, that we will not be alone as we cross from this life to the next. God will be with us. His rod and staff will guide us and protect us even in the valley of the shadow of death.

There are certainly unknowns about death and the afterlife, but the things we do know assure us that we won't be alone on that journey.

A Hiding Place

The LORD is good, a refuge in times of trouble. He cares for those who trust in him.
Nahum 1:7

A refuge. That's what we all want, isn't it? When the burdens of life weigh down on us and we can't find relief, we just want to run away and hide. What is a refuge? A safe place. A protected place. A hiding place. God is available to be all those things to us in our times of discouragement.

But the second sentence of this verse is very important. He's available for those who trust in Him. Trust is an interesting thing because it means believing God is there and that He's working, even when you can't actually see what He's doing. Trust Him to take care of you and those you love, then He will truly be your refuge.

Amazing Love

How great is the love the Father has lavished on us, that we should be called children of God!
1 John 3:1

Parent/child relationships are sometimes difficult. Often, parents want to do everything for their children, from giving them whatever they can to solving all their problems. However, good parents know that sometimes children have to go through difficult times in order to learn valuable lessons and children simply can't have everything they want. It wouldn't be good for them. That shows how much the parent really loves the child.

You are God's child and He showers you with His love – that doesn't mean He gives you everything you think you need. But if you stop and think about all He does for you, and all He does give you, you will know that you are totally, completely loved.

Fighting Discouragement

*A heart at peace gives life to
the body, but envy rots the bones.*
Proverbs 14:30

Why do you struggle with discouragement? What is it that gets you down? Are you looking around at friends and seeing that they have bigger houses, nicer cars, more impressive careers and more successful children? Do you find yourself longing for some of the things your friends have? If so, you're setting yourself up for discouragement.

A heart at peace is content (of course it aspires to continue to grow and improve) and does not envy others. Being at peace actually assists the growing/ improving process because you can achieve more when you're not discouraged or frantically racing around trying to grab more out of life.

Let your heart be at peace and defeat discouragement. You'll be glad you did.

Power Living

*I pray also that the eyes of your heart may be
enlightened in order that you may know the hope
to which he has called you, the riches of his
glorious inheritance in the saints, and his
incomparably great power for us who believe.*
Ephesians 1:18-19

In our discouragement, we sometimes get stuck in tunnel vision. All we can see before us are the things that are wrong in our lives. We know we don't have the power to change those things ... they are simply out of our hands. So we get discouraged.

Paul's prayer for the Ephesians has a message for us, too. Pray that the eyes of your heart will be opened to the inheritance you have as God's child. Remember how God has worked on your behalf in the past and that His power, His great power is available to you today.

Breaking the Cycle

*Praise the LORD, O my soul, and forget not all his
benefits – who forgives all your sins and heals
all your diseases, who redeems your life from
the pit and crowns you with love and compassion,
who satisfies your desires with good things
so that your youth is renewed like the eagle's.*

Psalm 103:2-4

"God, do this. Fix that. Guide me, show me, help me." Does your discouragement stem from what God doesn't do? Do you make plans for your life, ask Him to bless them, then get discouraged because He doesn't do what you want Him to do?

The psalmist encourages you to remember what God does for you every day. Read through this list, stop and meditate on each of God's loving acts. When your mind is filled with these good memories, perhaps the discouragement cycle will break as you praise and love God.

Memories

*The LORD your God has blessed you in all
the work of your hands. He has watched
over your journey through this vast desert.
These forty years the LORD your God has been
with you, and you have not lacked anything.*

Deuteronomy 2:7

Moses spoke these words to the Hebrews to remind
them of God's miraculous works on their behalf.
The Hebrews had a habit of quickly forgetting
God's work and sliding back into their pattern
of complaining about their situation – they got
discouraged. Moses knew it would help them to
focus on God's goodness and care.

If you're struggling with discouragement, why
not try Moses' remedy? Step back and remember
how God has blessed you and cared for you. Has
He let you lack for anything? Has He blessed your
work? Hold on to those things and move forward
trusting Him.

Rest for the Weary

*"Come to me, all you who are weary
and burdened, and I will give you rest."*
Matthew 11:28

What an offer this is! Jesus offers us a respite from the heavy load of discouragement. Close your eyes and imagine Him standing before you, arms outstretched, beckoning you to come to Him. You walk toward Him and with each step you can feel the weight lifting from your shoulders. It's a good mental picture, isn't it?

Jesus especially calls those who are worn out from carrying heavy burdens. He knows that they most need what He has to offer. Perhaps you are one whom He is calling. Are you ready to take the first step toward Him? The promise of rest is pretty enticing, isn't it? Let go of your discouragement and go to Him. You'll be glad you did.

Never Alone

The LORD upholds all those who
fall and lifts up all who are bowed down.
Psalm 145:14

What do you want most when you're discouraged? Relief from the discouragement? The knowledge that someone cares about you? Where do you turn to find this? If you are searching for it from friends or loved ones, you may be disappointed. The empathy of other people can only go so far.

But if you take your pain and discouragement to the Lord, stay quiet before Him, and wait for Him, you will find what you're looking for. He is the only One who can truly lift you up. He loves you very much. He cares about the heavy load you're carrying. He may not take your problems away, but He will walk with you through them. You are not alone. Go to Him, wait quietly before Him, sense His love.

Obey Always

Be strong and very courageous. Be careful
to obey all the law my servant Moses gave you;
do not turn from it to the right or to the left,
that you may be successful wherever you go.

Joshua 1:7

God's people have no reason to be defeated or discouraged. His power and strength are available to us. His command to Joshua in this verse is repeated three times in the first chapter of Joshua. *Be strong and courageous.*

What can defeat you when God is working for you? But there is a stipulation in this verse, too. Be careful to obey – all the time – to the best of your ability. If you're discouraged about failures in your life, stop and consider whether or not you've been obedient to God's laws. Don't expect God to bless you if you aren't obeying Him to the fullest extent of your knowledge and ability.

Rumble or Humble

Humble yourselves, therefore, under God's
mighty hand, that he may lift you up in due time.
1 Peter 5:6

Arrogance and pride will get you nowhere. If you approach life thinking that you know best and that you've got things under control, you're going to have problems. People who live that way tell God, "Hey, I'll call you if I need you, otherwise ... hands off!" Well, that, my friends, is not what God wants to hear.

What does it mean to humble yourself before God? It means letting go of the controls, bowing your head and heart before Him and waiting for His leading and direction. So, acknowledge that God is guiding and leading you. You can trust Him. If you humble yourself before Him, He will lift you up. You will know that you're in good hands.

Learn and Grow

We know that in all things God works
for the good of those who love him, who
have been called according to his purpose.
Romans 8:28

When you're stuck in discouragement it's hard to imagine that anything good can come from what you're going through. Sometimes it's even hard to imagine that God would allow these things to happen.

This verse is sometimes misquoted or at least misinterpreted. It doesn't say that God makes bad things good. It does say that in all situations He works *for* the good. There are lessons to be learned and character qualities to be developed in each situation. If you love Him and are obeying Him, then ask Him to work for good in your difficult situation. Learn and grow from it. Make it count for something. You'll be a better person and a stronger child of God for it.

The Great Physician

He heals the brokenhearted
and binds up their wounds.
Psalm 147:3

The universe is so big. There are so many crisis situations. There are so many people with serious problems. Do you sometimes feel as if your measly little problems couldn't possibly be that important to God? At the same time, though, you just want to matter to Him, right? You just want to know that He cares about you and what you're going through. He does.

Read through the Psalms and you will find verses like this one over and over. God cares about you. He cares when you're hurting. He will help you. He will mend your broken heart. He will bandage your wounds. He will help you move forward.

The Big Picture

"Do not let your hearts be troubled. Trust in God;
trust also in me. In my Father's house are many
rooms: if it were not so, I would have told you.
I am going there to prepare a place for you."
John 14:1-2

Discouragement makes you focus on the moment. You get stuck on the pain, the hopelessness or the loneliness in your heart. You can't seem to see a light at the end of the tunnel or if you do, you fear it's a train rushing toward you. Trust becomes a lost element of your walk with God. There's no future in that.

Allow God to remind you that the hard times won't last forever. He has an incredible future planned for you. Know that if He's gone to all that trouble to plan eternity, He's going to take care of today, too. Trust Him.

Precious

For he will deliver the needy who cry out, the
afflicted who have no one to help. He will take pity
on the weak and the needy and save the needy
from death. He will rescue them from oppression
and violence, for precious is their blood in his sight.
Psalm 72:12-14

If you skim through this verse you'll miss a very important word – precious. Imagine being precious to the Creator! You are.

At one time or another we have all been aware of the conditions mentioned here in our lives. This verse affirms that each of us is precious to God. He cares whether even a single drop of your blood is spilled. Your life is precious to Him. Savor that thought for a minute. The almighty God, who has the weight of the world shouting for His attention, thinks you are precious. Makes you feel pretty special, doesn't it?

Blessings

*"Blessed are the poor in spirit, for theirs
is the kingdom of heaven. Blessed are
those who mourn, for they will be comforted."*
Matthew 5:3-4

Does it seem to you that the strong, powerful people of the world are the ones who succeed in life? They seem to be in positions of authority, and have influence over others. They set the standard for the rest of us.

But Jesus said in the Beatitudes that in the big picture the humble and meek will be blessed. Those who mourn loved ones will be comforted. Jesus preferred to spend time with the not-so-powerful, the not-so-influential people of His world. He knew that those who were hurting would seek Him out more readily than those who felt self-sufficient. So, if you're hurting today, turn to Jesus. He promised you comfort, blessings and the hope of heaven.

Dark Nights

*No one will be able to stand up against you all
the days of your life. As I was with Moses, so I will
be with you; I will never leave you nor forsake you.*

Joshua 1:5

Do you have trouble sleeping when something
is weighing on your mind? Do you find yourself
pacing the floor half the night, unable to quiet your
racing mind? If so, you know how dark the night
gets just before dawn. In that quiet dark you can
feel so alone with your problems.

Just as God promised to be with Joshua all the
days of his life, He is with you. He promises to never
leave you or forsake you. Even if at this moment
you can't sense His presence, be assured that God
is with you. He knows what you're going through
and He cares.

Behind the Scenes

*He is the image of the invisible God, the
firstborn over all creation. For by him all
things were created: things in heaven and on
earth, visible and invisible, whether thrones or
powers or rulers or authorities; all things were
created by him and for him. He is before
all things, and in him all things hold together.*

Colossians 1:15-17

Christ is the image of God Himself. He was before all things and He is what holds all things together. Christ was involved in the creation of all things and all earthly powers.

Why are we reviewing these well-known facts, you ask? Because Christ who has all power, knowledge and wisdom can take care of you. Whatever is knocking you down is not too big for Him. Take your problems to Him, rest in Him. You don't have to worry about things anymore. Trust Him to take care of you.

The Great Comforter

Praise be to the God and Father of our
Lord Jesus Christ, the Father of compassion
and the God of all comfort, who comforts
us in all our troubles, so that we can
comfort those in any trouble with the comfort
we ourselves have received from God.
2 Corinthians 1:3-4

Being a child of God doesn't mean you won't have difficult times in life. He does, however, walk with us through the hard times. Frankly, He loves you so much that He hurts when you hurt. Because of that compassion, He promises to comfort you when your heart is breaking.

How does God show comfort? Sometimes through people in your life, sometimes through a sense deep in your soul that He loves you. When you experience God's comfort, you can show comfort and compassion to others – bring God's comfort to them.

Victory!

*The LORD said to Joshua, "Do not be afraid
of them; I have given them into your hand.
Not one of them will be able to withstand you."*

Joshua 10:8

Sometimes it feels as if life is out of control. Things happen so quickly that you can't grab on anywhere. A familiar panic begins to grow in your stomach and color every moment of every day. Perhaps you are afraid that no one is really in control. Perhaps it seems that the bad guys are winning.

Well, in the long run the bad guys will not win. God told Joshua that he shouldn't be afraid and you also have the assurance that in the final chapter, God is the victor, and you're on His team.

So, whatever weighs on you today, you have nothing to fear. You're already assured of victory.

Certainty

He who avenges blood remembers;
he does not ignore the cry of the afflicted.
Psalm 9:12

As you read through the psalms you hear the psalmist's cry to God over and over again. He questions why God is silent, why He doesn't seem to hear or to answer the heartfelt cries of the writer.

Do you feel like that sometimes? You pour out your heart to God, begging to hear His voice and know His response to your prayer and it seems that all you hear is ... silence. That's hard, isn't it? In this psalm of praise David reminds you to praise God because He does hear your prayers. He does remember you and care about what you're going through. In His time He *will* answer. You can know that for certain as you wait on Him.

Future Joy

*The ransomed of the LORD will return. They
will enter Zion with singing; everlasting joy will
crown their heads. Gladness and joy will overtake
them, and sorrow and sighing will flee away.*

Isaiah 35:10

In this description of the victorious return of God's people to Jerusalem, we read of exuberant and overwhelming joy. Have you ever been so filled with joy that you are overcome and you can't find words to express yourself?

The joy of the Israelites mentioned here is just a hint of the joy ahead for you. God has delivered you from the bondage of sin and the joy of heaven awaits. The sorrow and sighing that fills your heart now will end one day. You will be overwhelmed with gladness and joy and the pain and discouragement of today will be forgotten.

Hanging in There

Blessed is the man who perseveres under
trial, because when he has stood the test,
he will receive the crown of life that
God has promised to those who love him.
James 1:12

When you're in the middle of a trial, the last thing you want to hear about is the joy of persevering ... hanging in there. When you're hurting, you just want the hurt to stop, right?

The reality is that very few people make it through life without times of discouragement, stress and pain. It's going to happen. The key is what you do when it does. You can cave in and become a sniveling, whining, defeated woman, or you can persevere. That means you keep on going, keep your chin up, don't give up. Doing so results in a prize you could never have imagined – the crown of life – God's reward for your perseverance.

How Do You Spell Relief?

*When my spirit grows faint within
me, it is you who know my way.*

Psalm 142:3

David wrote this psalm from a cave where he was hiding from those who wanted to kill him. Life doesn't get much more stressful than that. We can learn quite a lesson from David. In this stressful, discouraging time of his life, he knew that God was in control. David didn't deserve to be hunted down, he had done nothing wrong. He had been anointed to be King of Israel. He was God's choice, but at the moment things weren't going well.

David didn't give up and get angry with God. He continually cried out to God for help. He knew that the answer to his problems was in God's hands. That's a good thing to remember.

Get Moving!

*See, the LORD your God has given you
the land. Go up and take possession of it
as the LORD, the God of your fathers, told
you. Do not be afraid; do not be discouraged.*
Deuteronomy 1:21

Is it possible that your discouragement comes from
lack of action? Perhaps you know something you
are supposed to be doing – a friend you should
witness to, a job you should take, a ministry you
should get involved in, a habit you should break –
something that requires you to take action; but you
don't. For whatever reason, you haven't gotten off
the couch and done a thing. Well, if you know that
to be true in your life, don't go complaining to God
about your discouragement. Show your trust in
Him. Get up and get busy and "take
the land God has given you." Put
work gloves on your faith and
get busy.

Big Picture

"I have loved you with an everlasting love;
I have drawn you with loving-kindness."
Jeremiah 31:3

We frail human beings get caught up in the moment. When we get so busy we can't sit or sleep or rest at all, when the burdens of life pile up on us and we can't see daylight, we forget the big picture.

What is the big picture, you ask? Simple – God loves us and draws us to Himself with incredible kindness. It's not a bad idea to remember that everything that happens to us in this life is simply a training ground for eternity, and eternity is what counts. So, step back from your problems and remember that God loves you. There is more to life than the burdens you're struggling with right now.

Mind Food

Finally, brothers, whatever is true, whatever is noble, whatever is right, whatever is pure, whatever is lovely, whatever is admirable – if anything is excellent or praiseworthy – think about such things.

Philippians 4:8

Garbage in, garbage out. What does that mean? Well, if you fill your physical body with junk food, it will become overweight and not very healthy. In the same way, if you fill your mind with negative, unkind, impure thoughts, it will show in your attitude and the way you treat other people. Fill your mind with true, noble, right, pure, lovely and admirable things and your attitude will be more positive, your energy levels will be higher, you will be more hopeful about life itself.

Where do you find these good things? In God's Word. Read it, absorb it and implant it in your mind. Let His Word guide your thoughts.

The Place to Start

Search me, O God, and know my heart;
test me and know my anxious thoughts.
See if there is any offensive way
in me, and lead me in the way everlasting.
Psalm 139:23-24

Discouragement happens and you just want it to stop. You can try all the positive thinking you want, you can try every formula for overcoming discouragement outlined in women's magazines, you can eat every chocolate bar within ten miles ... and still be discouraged.

A better place to begin the battle is found in this verse. Prayer. Allow God to search your heart, with nothing held back. Allow Him to show you what is below the surface, beneath the fine Christian veneer you wear for all to see. Ask God to reveal the sin in your heart, ask Him to lead you away from it. He will, and you'll be the better for it.

JUNE

A Powerful Prayer Life

Back-Up

When I called, you answered me;
you made me bold and stouthearted.

Psalm 138:3

"I'm calling for back-up!" TV show cops often announce that to the bad guys, and the bad guys shake in their boots. They know they are done for because the back-up guarantees they will be caught. The ability to call for back-up gives the single police officer courage because he knows he isn't alone. He has help to do his work.

When you turn to God and cry out for His help, you can be encouraged and strengthened by the knowledge that you have back-up. You aren't alone in your struggles. He will answer you with His guidance and awareness of His love. That should give you courage and determination in whatever is before you.

Follow-Through

This is the confidence we have in approaching God: that if we ask anything according to his will, he hears us. And if we know that he hears us – whatever we ask – we know that we have what we asked of him.

1 John 5:14-15

Teenagers are not always the most dependable in seeing things through – at least things their parents ask them. A simple request such as, "Could you put the trash out for pick up?" will usually result in "Yeah." But somehow it just doesn't happen. The teen's intentions were good ... but things got in the way of his follow-through.

We never have to worry about lack of follow-through from God. When we talk to Him, He hears us and when we make requests of Him, according to His will, and in obedience to Him, He will follow through in helping us. He promised.

Strong Foundation

Look to the Lord and his
strength; seek his face always.
1 Chronicles 16:11

Where do you turn when you need strength or help? Some people turn to substances – drugs, tranquilisers, alcohol, or food. Some people turn to friends. Friends encourage us in life and sometimes God uses them to guide us. But the best place we should turn – the first place to turn – is to God.

He is dependable and constant. His motives are always pure – to help us become more obedient and to grow in our service to Him. While others may have more selfish goals or may waver in their support of us, God's strength is a foundation of rock beneath us. Our goal should be to constantly be looking to Him, seeking His face for our guidance, encouragement, and strength.

Generous Giver

*"Ask and it will be given to you; seek and you will
find; knock and the door will be opened to you.
For everyone who asks receives; he who seeks finds;
and to him who knocks the door will be opened."*
Matthew 7:7-8

The look of sheer joy on a child's face when she tears
open a package and finds exactly what she wanted
delights a parent's heart. When you love someone,
you enjoy doing things for them and giving them
gifts and helping them. When someone you care
about has a need, all they have to do is ask and you
will quickly go to their aid.

God wants to help you, too. It's important to
recognize your need for Him and your dependence
on Him. When you turn to Him and admit your
need for help, guidance and wisdom, He'll be there.

You can count on it.

Giving Credit

*Help us, O God our Savior, for the
glory of your name; deliver us and
forgive our sins for your name's sake.*
Psalm 79:9

The best way to ensure that coworkers, friends or family will not want to help you with anything is to take personal credit for when they do assist you – and completely ignore any contribution they made. It's no fun to be taken for granted or to be completely ignored.

Keep that in mind when asking God for help. When you plead for His guidance, protection or intervention in your life and He gives it, give Him the credit. Use His answers to prayer as an opportunity to praise Him. Then people around you will see the evidence of His personal involvement in your life. It will be a testament to His love.

Spreading the Good News

*Pray for us that the message of
the Lord may spread rapidly and
be honored, just as it was with you.*
2 Thessalonians 3:1

Good news spreads quickly. When a college girl gets engaged, it's not long before the entire dorm hears the news and rush to see the ring. The message of God's love should spread even more quickly.

The apostle Paul felt that urgency. He wanted it to flow like a rushing river. He believed that prayer was vital to sharing the gospel successfully.

Remember to support your pastor, Sunday school teachers and missionaries in their efforts to spread the good news. Request prayer from your circle of supporters so that you will be able to share the gospel with people you meet.

Help Me!

*Immediately the boy's father exclaimed,
"I do believe; help me overcome my unbelief!"*
Mark 9:24

This is a powerful, honest prayer. No matter how long we've known the Lord, there is always room for our faith to grow stronger. We run up against situations when our faith may falter and we can't seem to connect with God. Deep down inside we know that we do believe; we just can't understand how the belief fits our current need.

The bottom line is that our faith is not negotiable. But we recognize that because of a certain crisis, our faith needs to grow. It's okay to admit that to God and to cry out in prayer, as this heartbroken father did, asking God to help your unbelief turn to belief. He will honor your honesty and answer your prayer.

Pray for Guidance

Teach me to do your will, for you are my God;
may your good Spirit lead me on level ground.
Psalm 143:10

Christianity isn't just about accepting Christ so your eternal destiny is settled; it's also about learning how to live your life.

God created people to live in community with others. Others may come to Him because they see His love in you. God will help you learn to live in love with others. His Word is your guidebook for learning how to relate to Him and to other people.

Your efforts to learn how God wants you to serve Him are fruitless unless you ask Him to teach you. Ask God to teach you His will for you – it's always a work in progress – changing and growing. Make sure all your efforts to know His will are bathed in prayer for His guidance.

Praise!

Praise the LORD. Praise God in his sanctuary;
praise him in his mighty heavens ... Let everything
that has breath praise the LORD. Praise the LORD.
Psalm 150:1; 6

"Give me ... I want ... give me, help me, give me."
How much of your time in prayer is spent in asking
God to do something, or help you with something?
Now think about how much of your prayers consist
of praise for who God is.

Is your prayer time so rushed that you feel you
must quickly get through your list of requests? Do
you take time to just meditate on who He is and
His creation, the evidence of His love for you; the
gift of His Word? There is so much to praise Him
for. Decide to put your requests at the end of your
prayer time. Praise Him first!

Power in Prayer

*I urge, then, first of all, that requests,
prayers, intercession and thanksgiving be
made for everyone – for kings and those
in authority, that we may live peaceful
and quiet lives in all godliness and holiness.*
1 Timothy 2:1-2

When a group of people get together it is not uncommon for some of them, for some of the time, to begin talking about politics and complaining about what the government is or isn't doing. This must have been common in Bible times, too, because Paul urged believers to pray for their leaders.

There is power in prayer and the way Christians can turn the world's attention toward God is by praying for the decisions our leaders make. Paul urged us to remember our leaders. By lifting them up to God, praying about the influences on them, and asking God to give them wisdom and discernment, we influence our own quality of life.

No Worries

Do not be anxious about anything, but in everything, by prayer and petition, with thanksgiving, present your requests to God.
Philippians 4:6

It's the middle of the night. Darkness blankets the room. You should be sleeping, but you're wide awake. Your mind races with concerns about what could happen. You're living in a land of "what ifs".

Sound familiar? Unfortunately, many of us regularly visit What If Land. But it isn't necessary. Much of what we worry about is out of our hands. They are situations we can't change – but God can. He invites us to bring our requests to Him and leave them there. We can know that He will take care of things, because He tells us not to worry. So, don't waste your energy on worrying; use it to praise God, thank Him for His care, and give your worries to Him.

Private Prayer

*"When you pray, go into your room,
close the door and pray to your Father
who is unseen. Then your Father, who
sees what is done in secret, will reward you."*

Matthew 6:6

When you settle down to pray, does your mind wander? Do you find yourself praying some, then making a mental list of things you need to do? This verse seems to have a dual purpose in teaching about prayer. We are not to publicly pray fancy prayers – just for show. We are also encouraged to withdraw from the busyness of our lives and concentrate as we pray.

Satan will try to disrupt your prayer time – that's a given. He may remind you to pick up the dry-cleaning or call your child's teacher – anything to pull your mind away from prayer. Don't do that! Give your full attention to God, shut out everything else. Enjoy God!

Just Ask

You do not have because you do not ask God.
James 4:2

There is an old expression that says, "You won't know if you don't ask." You won't know if another person will do something for you or give you something if you don't ask them. The other person may not know the intensity of your desire or even know of your specific need until you ask them for help.

Prayer is the way we communicate our requests to God. Of course, He knows what we need before we even ask Him, but *we* may not really know until we formulate the words in our hearts. Think about what you want God to do for you and what you want Him to teach you. Then, ask Him. He's waiting to help you.

Family Prayers

*Pray in the Spirit on all occasions with all kinds of
prayers and requests. With this in mind, be alert
and always keep on praying for all the saints.*
Ephesians 6:18

Belonging to a team or a family unit means you have
the support of the other members. Sometimes that
support is what keeps you going when you don't
feel that you can take another step.

You experience that same kind of support from
the family of God. Each of us should be in constant
prayer for one another, lifting up and encouraging
one another every day. Be alert to those around you,
sense their needs, and constantly bring them before
the Lord. They will do the same thing for you – you
can't fall too far, no matter what happens, when
you know your brothers and sisters are holding
you before the Lord. What power!

Forgive and Forget

*"Forgive us our sins, for we also
forgive everyone who sins against us."*
Luke 11:4

This verse comes straight from the example Jesus gave of the correct way to pray. He taught that it is important to ask God's forgiveness on a daily basis. It's tempting to scoot right over this in our prayer time and head right to the "meat" of our prayer, which is generally the requests we want God to hear and answer.

But why should He grant our requests if we aren't obeying Him? The tricky part is that none of us can obey all the time – that's beyond human capability. So, remember to calm your heart and mind as you begin praying, confess your sins and shortcomings and ask His forgiveness. Then ask for His strength to help you forgive those who have wronged you. Forgive and forget.

Praying for the World

*Your prayers and gifts to the poor have
come up as a memorial offering before God.*
Acts 10:4

Are you a prayer snob? Do you pray only for your friends or family members or people who are, for the most part, just like you? Are you impatient with the less fortunate in the world? Particularly impatient with those who (you think) could work a bit harder to make their own lot in life better? If so ... shame on you!

Paul tells us in this verse that our concern through prayer and actual gifts to the poor is a pleasant offering to God. He is pleased when we are concerned enough about others, even other people groups, to pray for them and when we give to help their living situations improve. We should lift up one another any way we can.

Praying in Belief

*"Whatever you ask for in prayer, believe that
you have received it, and it will be yours."*

Mark 11:24

Trust the One to whom you pray. You can pray for hours and hours, using the fanciest five-dollar words you can think of, but if you don't believe that God hears your prayers and that He has the power and authority to answer them ... you're wasting your time and energy.

Proper praying begins with spending time in God's Word and aligning your will with His. That means you basically want the same things out of life. Then, when you pray, you can believe that God will answer you. He's waiting to give you the desires of your heart. So, learn about Him, know Him, pray to Him and trust Him. You'll be glad you did!

Forgive and Pray

*"When you stand praying, if you hold anything
against anyone, forgive him, so that your
Father in heaven may forgive you your sins."*
Mark 11:25

Don't ask for something you aren't willing to give.
It's pointless to ask God to forgive your sins if
you are not willing to forgive someone who has
wronged you. No one goes through life without
touching other lives. You have to work with others
and usually live around others.

Once in a while, either on purpose or accidentally,
someone may wrong you. You can grab that wrong
and hold on to it. You can nurse it until it grows to
a big wrong in your mind. But if you're going to do
that, how could you dare to ask God to forgive your
sins? Be willing to show the same kind of grace to
others that you want God to show to you.

Power!

*The prayer of a righteous
man is powerful and effective.*
James 5:16

"I wish there was something I could do." Do you sometimes think that when you see someone suffering or experiencing a difficult time?

Well there is something you can do. Pray. Prayer makes a difference. God promises that our prayers are powerful and effective. However, there is one word in James 5:16 that cannot be overlooked – *righteous*. It's important when we come before God to confess our sins and ask forgiveness. Then we stand before Him clean and righteous. It's also important to live our lives in obedience to Him.

We can't do what we want, then expect Him to do what we want Him to do. Live as righteously as possible, confess your sins, then pray with all your heart. It makes a difference.

When You Can't Pray

*We do not know what we ought to pray for,
but the Spirit himself intercedes for us with
groans that words cannot express. And he
who searches our hearts knows the mind
of the Spirit, because the Spirit intercedes
for the saints in accordance with God's will.*

Romans 8:26-27

Sometimes the pain is so deep that we can't even pray. We want God to make the pain stop – heal the disease – repair the relationship – restore the job. But deep down inside we know that may not be what God wants – and so we don't know what to pray.

When our hearts are at a loss for the right words the Spirit takes over. He lives within our hearts and He cries out to God for us. So, when you can't find the words, be comforted that the Holy Spirit is interceding for you, and God hears His prayers.

Love One Another

"May they be brought to complete unity to let the world know that you sent me and have loved them even as you have loved me."
John 17:23

Jesus prayed for us ... His followers. He wanted us to live in unity – to get along. He knew that non-believers would be drawn to us and to Him by the love they see in our lives. How can we tell them about God's love for them if they see us fighting and scrapping with our Christian brothers and sisters? Nearly every church experiences times when the members don't get along.

Sometimes the struggles between denominations become public. That must make Satan smile. Join Jesus in praying for unity among believers ... even across denominational lines. Pray that we will stand strong together, as evidence of His love for the entire world.

Being Teachable

Show me your ways, O Lord, teach me your paths;
guide me in your truth and teach me, for you are
God, my Savior, and my hope is in you all day long.
Psalm 25:4-5

With a baby's first steps, a whole new world opens up to explore, with many lessons to be learned. It's the same for believers as we learn to live the Christian life. The foundation for those lessons is to be on our knees, when we ask the Lord to show us how to live and what path to follow in life.

A key part of this is found at the end of verse 5 – all day long. It's important to patiently wait for God's guidance instead of plowing ahead in life. We must be quiet before Him ... for a while ... to let our minds and hearts settle down and hear His guidance.

Fully Equipped

May the God of peace ... equip you with everything good for doing his will, and may he work in us what is pleasing to him, through Jesus Christ, to whom be glory for ever and ever. Amen.
Hebrews 13:20-21

"I can't do it, God!" "This is too hard." "I don't know how!" Have you ever felt like this? God will give you the words, actions, thoughts, and abilities you need to do the work He gives you to do. He doesn't send you into the world unequipped.

Pray for yourself and for others, asking God to give you all you need to do His work. Don't minimize the skills and talents He gives, just remember to give the glory to Jesus Christ for any gifts or talents God gives you, and get busy doing His work!

Always Special!

Keep me as the apple of your eye;
hide me in the shadow of your wings.

Psalm 17:8

The "apple of your eye" presents kind of an unusual mental image, doesn't it? When someone is the apple of your eye, it means they are special and precious to you. You delight in them.

The wonderful thing about the psalmist's words is that they confirm that you are the apple of God's eye – you're special to Him! So special that He will hide you under His wings just as a mother hen gathers her chicks under her wings, hiding them from view and protecting them from any dangers. Run to Him, trusting in His concern and love for you and allow Him to protect you from the cares of the world.

First Step

*Then I acknowledged my sin to you and
did not cover up my iniquity, I said, "I
will confess my transgressions to the LORD" –
and you forgave the guilt of my sin.*

Psalm 32:5

Electric currents rush through wires to light your
home, make your radio or TV play ... unless there
is a break in the wires. If anything blocks the lines,
the power is broken.

Your relationship with the Lord is like this, too.
Before you come to Him with praise for who He
is, His power, His love and strength ... before you
bring your requests to Him, asking His intervention
and help ... before you speak any other words to
Him – confess. Admit your own shortcomings and
sins and ask His forgiveness. Then you can come
to Him, cleansed by the blood of Jesus, pure
in the sight of God.

Confess then Praise

Praise the LORD, O my soul; all my inmost being, praise his holy name.
Psalm 103:1

It feels good to hear someone say nice things about you, doesn't it? It lifts your spirits, encourages you and gives you confidence.

Now, God doesn't need our encouragement or affirmation, but He does delight in our praise. Why? Because as we praise Him, we focus on His character and attributes. Taking time in our prayer life to think about the power, awesomeness, compassion and love of God results in our praise of Him and that encourages us.

Strange, isn't it? We give Him praise and we end up feeling closer and more loving to Him because we remember how wonderful He is. So, after you've confessed your sin to Him, praise Him for all that He is!

Powerful Faith

"If you have faith and do not doubt ... you can say to this mountain, 'Go throw yourself into the sea, and it will be done. If you believe, you will receive whatever you ask for in prayer.'"
Matthew 21:21-22

Is your faith strong? Think about this – scientists say that we use only a miniscule portion of our brains. If we could figure out how to harness the potential of our brains, there is no telling what we could achieve.

This is even more true of our faith. Our prayers could be so powerful that a mountain would throw itself into the sea if only our faith were strong enough. Bring your requests to God, and as you do ask Him to help your faith grow and grow and grow. There is no limit to what praying in real faith can accomplish!

Urgent Need

*"The harvest is plentiful but the workers
are few. Ask the Lord of the harvest, therefore,
to send out workers into his harvest field."*
Matthew 9:37-38

Hell is a real place. There are people in this world right now who will spend eternity in hell. Sometimes that truth gets muddled up and lost in our concept of a loving God. God is loving, but He has laid out the guidelines for entering His heaven and He isn't going to change His mind.

We should sense His urgency to spread the gospel to the entire world. Perhaps God hasn't called you to go to a foreign country ... but you can pray. Pray that God will call workers to spread the Good News. Pray that those whom He calls will answer that call. Pray with urgency.

Scripture Prayers

Let the word of Christ dwell in you richly as you teach and admonish one another with all wisdom, and as you sing psalms, hymns and spiritual songs with gratitude in your hearts to God.

Colossians 3:16

Pray the words of Scripture. What better way to gain understanding of God's Word than to memorize it and pray it back to God. As you do this, He will open your heart to the possibilities of knowing Him and absorbing His Words into your heart.

You can pray God's promises to Him because they are just that – promises He gives you as to how He wants to work in your heart and life. You can be assured that you are praying in His will when you are praying God's own words. Spend time reading and learning His Word, then joyfully pray in God's own words!

Prayer for Growth

May my cry come before you, O LORD;
give me understanding according to your word.
Psalm 119:169

It's so much fun to watch a child discover the world around her. Blowing the fuzzies of a dandelion, playing with a puppy, watching fish swim ... the joy of discovery is part of growing up.

We should know the same kind of joy as our relationship with God grows. We should never feel that we know all there is to know about God; we understand Scripture as much as we ever will; we walk in faith as much as possible. It's just not true. Ask God ... no, *cry out* to God to increase your understanding and grow your faith. Don't ever be content with your Christian walk – strive to grow closer and closer to Him!

JULY

When Things Go Wrong

Hold Your Horses

Wait for the LORD; be strong and
take heart and wait for the LORD.
Psalm 27:14

Do you know the phrase, "Like a bull in a china shop"? Does the way you live your life illustrate that phrase? Do you feel that you're in a constant state of crisis, running around, wildly attacking those problems ... without even seeking God's guidance? Sometimes problems are times of learning. However, if you blindly rush from potential solution to potential solution – as you see them – you may miss the lesson.

Take this verse to heart ... slow down ... stop ... trust God and wait for Him to act. He hasn't forgotten you or what you're going through. He *will* guide and lead. Wait on Him.

Unbreakable!

We are hard pressed on every side,
but not crushed; perplexed, but not in despair.
2 Corinthians 4:8

"God, I can't take much more of this! I'm at the end of my rope here. Are You even paying attention?" When it feels like life is closing in on you and God is nowhere to be found, it's time to look at the history of God's dealings with His people. Look back through Scripture – did He ever turn His back when His people needed Him? He didn't.

Look back at your own history with Him. Hasn't He always been there when you needed Him? Of course He has. So, no matter how hard pressed you are; or how perplexed you may feel, trust Him to keep you from being crushed or pushed to the point of despair. Remember ... He loves you.

A Sure Thing

*Those who know your name will
trust in you, for you, LORD, have
never forsaken those who seek you.*

Psalm 9:10

Stress is a terrible thing. It can eat away at you until you have no peace, no joy and no ability to see good in anything. It robs you of sleep, health, and enjoyment. It chips away at your relationship with God and your self-image. Yes, stress is a powerful tool that Satan uses to pull God's people away from Him.

What's the antidote to stress? It's right here in this verse ... trust. There are very few sure things in this world, but God's love for His people is a definite sure thing. He can be trusted. He never (did you get that – *never*) forsakes those who seek Him. So, what's the antidote to stress? Seek Him!

Standing Firm

Moses answered the people, "Do not be afraid. Stand firm and you will see the deliverance the LORD will bring you today."
Exodus 14:13

Have you ever tried the test of courage where someone claps her hands right in front of your eyes while you try with all your strength not to blink? It's almost impossible not to react. Do you have a similar reaction when you see problems building in your life?

The natural reaction is to scurry around, frantically trying to stave off the problem or solve it yourself. But that's not what Moses told the Israelites to do in their crisis. He encouraged them to stand firm. When they did, they saw God do a miracle! Take Moses' advice; stop the frantic activity, stop the noise. Just stop ... stand firm, (don't back away) and see what God will do for you.

Rest for Your Soul

*"Come to me, all you who are weary
and burdened, and I will give you rest."*
Matthew 11:28

"If I can just hang on for a few more weeks, then I'll take a vacation." Have you ever said that? The truth is that no matter where you go, your problems and stresses eventually come along for the ride.

You can look for solutions in your friendships, career, "stuff" or a multitude of other places. None of them will offer permanent solutions – only Jesus will. He promises to give you rest from all that is weighing you down. All you have to do is come to Him. So let go of the other things. Just come to Jesus. That's simple enough, right?

Me Against the World

He will deliver the needy who cry out,
the afflicted who have no one to help.
Psalm 72:12

"My son drops every piece of clothing he touches on the floor ... and leaves them there." "Stacks of mail accumulate on the kitchen counter ... because my husband *needs* to look at each piece." "My daughter's room looks like someone picked it up and shook it." "I feel like it's me against them!" The constancy of these kinds of problems brings a daily kind of stress.

Of course, there are also problems which have much more serious consequences. Whether you are dealing with the daily stresses of life, or stresses with serious consequences, it's comforting to know you aren't alone. God promises to deliver those who cry out to Him ... especially those who seem to be standing alone.

Flexible Strength

Be strong and courageous. Do not be terrified;
do not be discouraged, for the LORD
your God will be with you wherever you go.
Joshua 1:9

Stress can make you panic and feel that there is no way out and that your problems will never end. Some people experience anxiety attacks because of the panic.

These words in Joshua remind us to be strong in the struggles of life. To understand this, think about a young tree struggling through a violent windstorm. The powerful gusts whip the tree back and forth, bending it so that it is nearly bent in half. It seems impossible that the little tree could stay rooted in the ground, but it does and it doesn't break. You can find that same kind of strength in the trials of life, because your God is with you.

A Shepherd's Love

*He tends his flock like a shepherd: He gathers
the lambs in his arms and carries them close to
his heart; he gently leads those that have young.*

Isaiah 40:11

A shepherd cares for his sheep. He protects them from predators. He makes sure they have food, water and a place to sleep. He rescues them from their own bad choices. He tenderly carries the young lambs. Everyone needs tenderness, especially when it feels like life is beating you up and people you thought you could trust have let you down.

Here's the answer to that need – God. Close your eyes, imagine Him holding you gently in His arms ... close to His heart, tenderly caring for you as a shepherd cares for a lamb. Whatever you're facing, whatever you're struggling through, whatever is weighing you down, know that you can rest in His loving arms.

Sustaining Strength

Cast your cares on the LORD and he will
sustain you; he will never let the righteous fall.
Psalm 55:22

Sustain – a word that implies strength and longevity.
If you, in the midst of your trial, give your cares to
the Lord, He will give you strength and endurance
to get through them. But don't miss the last phrase
of this verse – it's speaking of the righteous. In order
to experience His sustaining strength, you must be
obedient to His truth. If you're living in some willy-
nilly-obey-when-you-feel-like-it manner, don't
expect His help. He upholds the righteous. Maybe
you think, "I don't have the strength to do any more
than I'm already doing!"

Well, don't fret. Do you long to know
God better? Do you spend time in His
Word and in prayer each day (even a
few minutes)? Then you're moving in
the right direction, so give Him your
cares.

Domino Effect

We know that suffering produces perseverance;
perseverance, character; and character, hope.
And hope does not disappoint us, because
God has poured out his love into our hearts
by the Holy Spirit, whom he has given us.
Romans 5:3-5

Have you ever seen a long row of dominoes set on end? When the first one is bumped it tumbles into the next and that one hits the next one, until they all fall. These verses are the domino effect in reverse. Suffering hurts, but good can come from it. Suffering makes you develop "stick-to-it-iveness".

Stop and appreciate the fact that you're making it through difficulties – you're getting up each morning and putting one foot in front of the other and doing what you have to do. That builds character and that encourages hope, which reminds us of God's love. Whatever you're going through, God walks beside you all the way.

A Hiding Place

God is our refuge and strength
an ever-present help in trouble.
Psalm 46:1

When a small child is afraid of a coming storm she will sometimes run and hide, covering her ears and eyes and settle into the place where she feels most safe. Often, that's under the arm of her mom or dad.

As we grow up, we're often too proud to admit fear or even to admit stress. We no longer have mom or dad to put their arms around us and tell us everything will be all right, so we try to push our way through trouble on our own. But wait, we don't have to do that. God is our refuge. We can run to Him, tell Him all our troubles, and trust Him to protect us ... always.

Future Joy

"You will grieve, but your grief will turn to joy."
John 16:20

Jesus knew that life on this earth would sometimes be difficult and discouraging. Jesus knew that we would get caught up in the struggles of relationships and earning a living. He knew we would make bad choices, suffer illnesses, bare the brunt of broken relationships and even suffer for our faith in God. Jesus knew that we would sometimes grieve ... and that's okay. But, in the midst of our grieving, Jesus reminds us that one day our grief will turn to joy.

If we have accepted Jesus as our Savior, we can *know* that our eternity is set – with Him. That truth will turn any grief to joy. So, when you go through difficult times, don't forget the big picture – things are going to get better.

Greater than Anything

*Great is the LORD and most worthy of
praise; his greatness no one can fathom.*

Psalm 145:3

So, you have a problem and you can't think about
anything else. Day and night that one thing is on
your mind as you try to decide what to do about
it. That one stressful thing affects every area of your
life. You are so caught up in it that you can't see
any good anywhere else. Perhaps you have forgotten the truth in this verse – the God you worship,
the God who loves you, is most worthy of praise ...
your praise.

Nothing is greater than He is. In fact, no one can
begin to understand His greatness. He is greater
than whatever problem you're facing, so talk with
Him about it and ask for His help. He can help ...
and He will.

Strong in Prayer

*Be joyful in hope, patient in
affliction, faithful in prayer.*
Romans 12:12

Three easy steps to go from despair to joy. Of course,
anyone who has been in despair knows that the
steps are never easy – the journey is never quick.
However, these three steps are the only path out of
your despair. They will help you get your mind off
your problems and move forward. Joy and patience
are important, and certainly make life more bearable.
But devotion to prayer is vitally important. Sometimes we pray for God's help when life gets tough
but if we don't see an immediate answer, we cut
back on prayer or give it up all together.

This verse tells us to grow stronger in
prayer because that strength will help
us get through the hard times. It plays
a vital part in keeping us close to God
and focused on Him.

Keep Your Focus

The LORD is my light and my salvation –
whom shall I fear? The LORD is the stronghold
of my life – of whom shall I be afraid?
Psalm 27:1

Constant stress can make you crazy. Yet, in our busy lifestyles there isn't really any way to avoid stress. We've created a monster, now we have to figure out how to hide from it.

Truthfully, there is only one way – turning your heart back to the stronghold of your life. When you focus on Him and His values, when you seek His direction for your life, you soon realize that the things you've been allowing to stress you aren't as important as you thought. The problem is that the urgent things shout louder than the really important things. Keep your focus and don't let the "stuff" of life turn your focus away from the Lord.

God's Care

*The Lord is close to the brokenhearted
and saves those who are crushed in spirit.*
Psalm 34:18

Sometimes stress is the result of real losses in life. When you've had a major loss in life such as losing a loved one; a long-term job (which sometimes means loss of a lifestyle); or losing your own good health, stress is almost inevitable. The psalmist certainly knew what this felt like. We read over and over in the psalms of the writer's cries to God for help, comfort and strength. The psalmist came to the conclusion that the Lord knows and cares about our pain. He stays close to us, showing His care and concern in many ways.

Look around you – has God placed good friends in your life to support you? Look at the other ways He shows Himself to you. Focus on those good things and thank Him for His care.

A Peaceful Place

*The peace of God, which transcends all
understanding, will guard your
hearts and your minds in Christ Jesus.*

Philippians 4:7

Peace. Do you long for peace in the midst of the chaos of life? Do you have a peaceful place to which you can go in your mind – a memory of a peaceful, happy time? Sometimes a short mental vacation is what keeps you going. God's peace is beyond all understanding. It is a quiet, still refuge in the midst of a raging storm ... and it is available to you.

God's peace will calm you even more than that peaceful memory that you sometimes turn to. But you need to be still, focus on God and His Word, then allow that peace to wash over you. Take the time ... you'll be glad you did.

Wait in Trust

"Be still, and know that I am God; I will be exalted among the nations, I will be exalted in the earth."
Psalm 46:10

Do you long for rest from your stressful life? Do you long for quietness and peace? Do you long to be rescued? You have to do only one simple thing ... be still. Perhaps you think you have been still, waiting for God's direction or intervention in your life. But think about your stillness. Do you sit, perched on the edge of your chair, ready to leap into action as soon as you think you know what God wants you to do? Or do you sit back, feet up, relaxed and trusting as you wait for God's voice to whisper in your heart.

Being still takes time and implies a willingness to wait on God. Sit back, let your mind rest, listen for God.

Nothing!

For I am convinced that neither death nor life,
neither angels nor demons, neither the
present nor the future, nor any powers,
neither height nor depth, nor anything else
in all creation, will be able to separate us from the
love of God that is in Christ Jesus our Lord.
Romans 8:38-39

Too much work to do. Too many bills to pay. Too little money. What causes the stress in your life? From relationship problems, to busyness, to work, to money … stress is not in short supply. Sometimes, in our own minds, we allow those stresses to pull us away from the awareness of God's love.

This verse reminds us that none of those things can separate us from His love. So, as you begin another stressful day, stop and remember that God loves you. Even if it seems that the "stuff" of life is winning … it isn't!

A Gift of God

Moreover, when God gives any man
wealth and possessions, and enables him
to enjoy them, to accept his lot and be happy
in his work – this is a gift of God. He seldom
reflects on the days of his life, because God
keeps him occupied with gladness of heart.
Ecclesiastes 5:19-20

Has God blessed you with a measure of wealth and a career you enjoy? Or are you unhappy with your lot in life and long for change? Either way, do you find yourself stressing about trying to hold onto what you have or daydreaming about what you don't have? Perhaps that means you are allowing your heart to be occupied with the wrong things.

If you focus your heart on thanking God for what you have and the blessings He gives you, He will fill your heart with gladness. Sounds like a good plan.

Never Alone

When you pass through the waters, I will be with you; and when you pass through the rivers, they will not sweep over you. When you walk through the fire, you will not be burned; the flames will not set you ablaze. For I am the Lord, your God, the Holy One of Israel, your Savior.

Isaiah 43:2-3

Too much! Life weighs down on you. There are problems everywhere you look. You fall to your knees and cry out to God that you simply can't take anymore. But as you gaze into the future, there seems to be no respite from the pressures. How do you make it through?

Remember that you are not alone. Nothing that happens to you surprises God. He knows every detail and even more importantly ... He walks beside you through the problems. He is God – nothing and no one is more powerful than He is.

No Worries

*"Who of you by worrying can
add a single hour to his life?"*
Matthew 6:27

Do you expend a lot of energy on worry? Do you fret about what might happen and mentally play out the scenarios of what might come if life takes you down various trails? Are you worrying about things over which you have no control? Why? Will your worry change anything? It doesn't have the power to add length to your life and it will detract from your quality of life.

Two wonderful gifts can help us through the stresses of life. First, we have prayer – we can talk with God about our worries. Second, we have His Word to remind us of His presence and power. So, even when you can't make any sense of what's happening, trust God's heart. He has a plan and He will see you through.

Strength and Praise

O my Strength, I sing praise to you; you,
O God, are my fortress, my loving God.
Psalm 59:17

Focus, focus, focus! The stresses and problems of life could be magnified by your own attitudes. Are you the kind of person who looks at a glass as half empty rather than half full? A negative attitude just breeds more negativity, doesn't it? Even when your problems are serious and real, lifting your heart to sing praises to God, your strength and your fortress, can help to lift the weight of the burden bearing down on you.

Praising God is a powerful reminder that you aren't alone. There is great comfort in knowing that God cares about your problems and He will help you through them.

Contentment

I have learned to be content whatever the circumstances. I know what it is to be in need, and I know what it is to have plenty. I have learned the secret of being content in any and every situation whether well fed or hungry, whether living in plenty or in want.
Philippians 4:11-12

The apostle Paul knew that contentment lays a blanket of peacefulness deep in the soul. It frees us from the need to constantly be striving for more and more. Sit back, close your eyes and think about the areas in your life where there is stress and anxiety. Do you lack contentment with your home, finances, possessions?

Outside circumstances change; often the dynamics of that change are out of our control. So how do we find contentment? By focusing on God ... knowing Him, obeying Him and loving Him.

What Will Last?

*Your word, O LORD is eternal; it stands
firm in the heavens. Your faithfulness
continues through all generations.*
Psalm 119:89-90

When it's all said and done, what will stand the
test of time? We spend so much time and energy
stressing over things ... often things over which we
have no control. We fret over what "might have
been". We live in "woulda-coulda-shoulda" land
and miss the value of what will really last. God's
Word is our guideline for life and it is eternal.
Through His Word we can know God. We read of
His faithfulness and love to His people.

The bottom line is that the things we spend so
much emotional energy on will one day end,
but God's Word will continue forever. We
can know His presence with us ... His
faithfulness ... forever.

Blessings

The LORD bless you and keep you; the
LORD make his face shine upon you
and be gracious to you; the LORD turn
his face toward you and give you peace.
Numbers 6:24-26

This blessing goes back to the time of Moses. Look at each phrase and let it sink into your heart. It calls God's blessings and protection upon you. It calls for an awareness of God's presence in your life – the light of His face shining on you and His face turned toward you – God is looking at you. Then, the frosting on the cake ... peace. God will give you peace in the chaos of life. Peace. Makes you wonder where all the stress is coming from, doesn't it?

God doesn't move – we do. We move our focus away from Him and put things that aren't so important in the forefront, thus sacrificing peace. Silly, isn't it?

Fear Not

"So do not fear, for I am with you; do not be dismayed, for I am your God. I will strengthen you and help you; I will uphold you with my righteous right hand."

Isaiah 41:10

Sometimes life is hard. Stressful financial conditions, loss of a job, serious health issues, rebellious children, broken relationships ... those things and others press in to demand our attention and energy. Much of the time our problems are things that friends and family can't fix. They may empathize and truly care, but because they can't actually do anything, we may feel that we're walking through deep waters alone.

Well, we're not. God's presence is constant. His strength is always present. He promises to hold us up and not let us fall farther than His hand can reach. We ... you ... are never out of God's reach.

Under His Wings

*He will cover you with his feathers, and
under his wings you will find refuge;
his faithfulness will be your shield and rampart.*

Psalm 91:4

"I want to crawl into a hole and pull it in after me!" Have you ever felt like shouting that as you ran away from life ... until you realized that there is no place you can hide from the pressures of life. There is only one safe place and that is under God's wings. When life starts pressing in on you, imagine yourself snuggled under His wings, like a baby chick that is safely protected from the wind, rain or predators. There is no safer place to be.

It's your choice to go to God and find refuge and peace or to stay out in the unprotected open where you will be tossed about by the stresses of life.

Maturity

*Consider it pure joy, my brothers, whenever you
face trials of many kinds, because you know that
the testing of your faith develops perseverance.
Perseverance must finish its work so that you may
be mature and complete, not lacking anything.*

James 1:2-4

As much as you may not want to hear it, the problems you're dealing with may have a purpose. Do these verses mean you should jump up and down with joy when problems come along? No, God doesn't expect us to celebrate problems ... but what comes from them.

Learning to walk with God and staying close to Him in difficult times helps our faith grow stronger. Making it through a difficult time helps us know that we can get through the next one and the next one. That's called perseverance and it helps our faith mature. Now that's something to be happy about.

Don't Worry

*"Therefore do not worry about tomorrow,
for tomorrow will worry about itself.
Each day has enough trouble of its own."*
Matthew 6:34

Sometimes we spend a lot of energy worrying about what "might" happen tomorrow. Those anticipatory worries pile on to what we have to deal with every day, making the load nearly unbearable. This verse encourages us to deal with life a day at a time. Take time each day to connect with God, search His Word and be silent before Him.

Turn to God for the strength to make it through each day and do your best to stay focused on the day before you. Don't worry about the future, just take life a day at a time and lean on God to make it through.

Perfect Peace

You will keep in perfect peace him whose
mind is steadfast, because he trusts in you.

Isaiah 26:3

A tornado ripping through a town can do incredible damage, demolishing houses, lifting cars into the air and tossing them like toys, ripping full-grown trees out of the ground. But right in the center of the tornado, in the eye, there is calm ... peace. That's amazing, and it kind of gives a picture of hope. Because, if that peace in the midst of the storm can happen in nature, God can do it for you, too.

In the midst of anxiety, stress and the chaos of your life, fix your mind on God and keep it there. Be absolutely stubborn about focusing on Him and He promises to give you peace, right there in the center of the storm.

AUGUST

Trusting God

Grasping the Love

*I pray that you, being rooted and established
in love, may have power, together with all
the saints, to grasp how wide and long
and high and deep is the love of Christ.*
Ephesians 3:17-18

It is virtually impossible to trust someone whom
you don't love. You will constantly be questioning
motives if you don't believe you are loved, too. That's
why Paul prayed that the Christians in Ephesus
would understand the depths of God's love. This
understanding comes through the Holy Spirit and
it is foundational to trusting God. Grasping the
extent of God's love lays the groundwork for you
to trust Him.

You know that someone who loves you that much
wants the very best for you. Pray that God
will begin to allow you to understand the
depths of His love and to help that understanding grow ever deeper.

Tug-of-War

*Trust in the LORD and do good; dwell in the land
and enjoy safe pasture. Delight yourself in the
LORD and he will give you the desires of your heart.*
Psalm 37:3-4

Have you ever played tug-of-war? You and your
teammates hold a rope and pull with all your might
against a team on the other end of the rope, which is
doing the same thing. It's a struggle of strength and
will. Do you do that with God? Are you struggling
against Him to have your way in your life? If so,
you probably are not trusting Him.

Trusting God means that your will for your life
is becoming aligned with His. You aren't struggling
to have your way because you have submitted to
Him. Then God will give you the desires of your
heart – more than likely that will be the desire to
know Him better and to serve Him fully.

A Great Stabilizer

Let us fix our eyes on Jesus, the author and perfecter of our faith, who for the joy set before him endured the cross, scorning its shame, and sat down at the right hand of the throne of God.
Hebrews 12:2

A gymnast stands on a four-inch wide balance beam and spins around ... without falling off! Then she continues her routine of jumping, flipping and dancing on the beam. How does she spin and not get dizzy? How does she know when she has done two rotations? "Simple," she says, "I just fix my eyes on an object in front of me. It's my stabilizer. I count my rotations by how many times I pass it." Yeah, simple. But an interesting lesson on trusting.

Fix your eyes on Jesus. Lock your eyes on Him, then He will be the stabilizing factor no matter what else goes on in your life.

The Only Safe Place

The eternal God is your refuge,
and underneath are the everlasting arms.
Deuteronomy 33:27

God is the only safe place to put your trust. Do you sometimes have your doubts about that? That's all right, but just review what you know about Him. Remember how He took care of His people in Scripture – time after time – even when they didn't really obey him or stay true to Him.

Now, review what He has done for you and your loved ones. Do you see a thread of His faithfulness running through your life? Can you recall times when you didn't know where He was, but as you look back, His care is obvious? God is trustworthy. You can run to Him and hide in His love. You can trust Him to hold you up with those amazingly strong arms, regardless of what comes into your life. You can trust Him because He loves you.

Have Your Way, God

"I am the Lord's servant," Mary answered. "May it be to me as you have said." Then the angel left her.
Luke 1:38

Picture this ... Young Mary, probably a teenager, is suddenly informed that she's going to have a baby. She knows the gossip this will bring since she isn't married. She knows this situation is going to cause problems, possibly even with her fiancé and her family.

What incredible trust Mary showed when she responded to the angel, essentially saying, "Whatever God wants is fine with me. I trust Him with my future and with my life." Could you do that? Could you say, "Okay, God, do whatever You want." Could you say it (and mean it) even if you couldn't logically see any way the situation could work out for your good? Could you trust Him that much?

Taste and Trust

*Taste and see that the L*ORD *is good; blessed
is the man who takes refuge in him. Fear the L*ORD*,
you his saints, for those who fear him lack nothing.*

Psalm 34:8-9

We don't hear much these days about fearing God. Instead, we talk about how God loves us and is our friend. But it's dangerous to forget His awesome power, His jealousy for our love and attention, and the coming accountability for who or what reigns in our hearts. What's awesome is that fearing God ... giving Him the respect He deserves, being in awe of Him, and recognizing His power, results in God giving us everything we need. (Notice that the verse does not say He gives us everything we want.)

Once we have tasted what God has to offer, why would we look anywhere else for fulfillment? Why wouldn't we trust Him?

Trust and Praise

*O Lord, you are my God; I will exalt
you and praise your name, for in
perfect faithfulness you have done
marvelous things, things planned long ago.*
Isaiah 25:1

Trust is a strange thing. You can't just decide to trust someone, even God, and, boom – it happens. You must believe that the person you're trusting is worthy of your trust. In those "silent times" when you can't seem to connect with God, it may be harder to trust Him. What's the remedy? Look back. Look through Scripture and see God's faithfulness to His people. Look back at how God has always been there in your life, even when you couldn't see His hand.

God is faithful and will continue working out the plans He laid out long ago. The better you know Him the more you will be able to trust Him because you will know His heart.

Second Chances

*Because of the LORD's great love we
are not consumed, for his compassions
never fail. They are new every
morning; great is your faithfulness.*
Lamentations 3:22-23

So you messed up big time. You wake up filled with regret and guilt. You feel so bad that you don't even want to face God. How can you keep asking Him to forgive you for the same sins you have confessed over and over, determined never to commit again. But before you knew it, you did them again.

How? Simple answer ... He loves you. As far as He is concerned, every day is a second chance for you, because His compassion is new every day. Wow! Since God loves you that much, you can certainly trust Him to stick with you ... every single day.

Who Is in the Driver's Seat?

Then Jesus declared, "I am the bread of life.
He who comes to me will never go hungry,
and he who believes in me will never be thirsty."
John 6:35

Do you believe this verse? Really believe it? Do you trust Jesus enough to believe that coming to Him means you will never want for anything? Jesus is promising to supply all your needs ... not your wants, but your needs. You will never again hunger for hope and love. You will never again thirst for meaning in your life.

Of course, the key to this is in the phrase *He who comes to me*. What does it mean to come to Jesus? It means letting go of your control of your life. It means putting Him in control, letting Him guide and direct you and trusting that He will do that in love.

The Safest Place

When I am afraid, I will trust in you. In God,
whose word I praise, in God I trust; I will not
be afraid. What can mortal man do to me?
Psalm 56:3-4

Have you ever been really afraid? Not the childish fear of a boogeyman under your bed, but fear of what the future holds or doesn't hold. Fear of what another person may or may not do. Fear that someone you trust is going to let you down. Where do you turn when fear starts to grab your heart and hold you captive?

The steadiest place in all of the universe is God. He never changes. He loves you unconditionally. He can be trusted. When you are afraid, trust God to protect you and care for you. Nothing can happen to you that He doesn't already know about.

Trusting Christ

*The Spirit of the LORD will rest on him – the
Spirit of wisdom and of understanding, the
Spirit of counsel and of power, the Spirit of
knowledge and of the fear of the LORD –
and he will delight in the fear of the LORD.*

Isaiah 11:2-3

This prophecy tells us a lot about Jesus, and understanding it inspires our trust in Him. Look at the characteristics described here. Jesus embodies all the wisdom and understanding of God. He has the Spirit of counsel and power. He has knowledge.

Think about that. He can counsel and direct our lives. We can trust Him because He is God. He can handle whatever life throws at us. We know He loves us, and these verses affirm that His wisdom, power and knowledge can be trusted.

No Fear!

If we are thrown into the blazing furnace,
the God we serve is able to save us from it,
and he will rescue us from your hand, O king.
But even if he does not, we want you to know,
O king, that we will not serve your gods or
worship the image of gold you have set up.
Daniel 3:17-18

When the rubber meets the road, where does your trust in God end up? You may never have to put your life on the line for your faith, as the boys in Daniel 3 did, but you will have other choices. Choosing honesty – telling the truth on your taxes; choosing purity in relationships; choosing to admit your faith, even if it might cost you the "respect" of peers.

Do you trust God to get you through these things? Do you love Him enough to take a stand and take the consequences?

Quiet Love

The LORD your God is with you, he is
mighty to save. He will take great delight
in you; he will quiet you with his love,
he will rejoice over you with his singing.

Zephaniah 3:17

Do you sometimes feel alone especially when you're in the middle of the struggles of life? You're not alone. God is with you, even if you are struggling so much that you can't sense His presence. How do you handle problems? Does your mind race back and forth looking for answers? Does your heart beat frantically and your breath come in short gasps?

God wants you to trust Him. He wants to settle you – quiet you. Rest in His love – and listen for the music of His delight.

No Worries

"Do not let your hearts be troubled.
Trust in God; trust also in me."
John 14:1

Jesus went on in this message to affirm that He is the way, the truth and the life. No one comes to the Father except through Him. He knew that life was going to be troubling sometimes. He knew we would have problems and that some of them would even come because of our faith in Him. He didn't say that He would take the problems away. He did say we could trust Him to walk through them with us. He wanted us to know that whatever happens, our faith and trust in Him is worth it.

We have the hope of heaven in our future and the promise of His help right now. When we keep our eyes on Him, there is no reason for worry.

Powerful Faith

"I tell you the truth, if you have faith as small as a mustard seed, you can say to this mountain, 'Move from here to there'; and it will move. Nothing will be impossible for you."
Matthew 17:20

Faith is the bottom line. If you believe who God is; what Christ did for you; if you believe God's power; if you believe the Bible – nothing is impossible for you. Faith is a powerful thing ... even a little bit of faith. Faith that is as tiny as a mustard seed – that's tinier than your littlest finger tip – can move a mountain. Unless you've been rearranging the Rocky Mountains, you probably haven't even begun to tap the possibilities of faith in Christ.

Faith and trust go hand in hand. Believe who He is, let your faith and trust in Him grow, and see what He will do through you!

The Bottom Line

*"Therefore I tell you, do not worry about your life,
what you will eat or drink; or about your body,
what you will wear. Is not life more important than food,
and the body more important than clothes?"*

Matthew 6:25

So much time and energy is spent worrying about the "stuff" of life. Seriously think about the time we expend on material things such as food, clothing, home and stuff to put inside our homes. We all worry about these things, but they are not what's really important in life. Our relationship with and service to God is truly more important than these things.

The bottom line question is whether we trust God to take care of these material things. Are we willing to live by His standards and with what He supplies for us and give our energy and time to more important things?

Heart Placement

Do not love the world or anything in the world. If anyone loves the world, the love of the Father is not in him.

1 John 2:15

You can't straddle the fence. You can't keep one foot in the world and put one foot in God's Kingdom. You'll split in two. Loving the world means placing supreme value in what people think of you. It means placing importance on what status you reach in your career; how much money you earn; how big your home is; how much jewelry you own ... well, you get the idea.

Loving the world and loving God cannot coexist. Being filled with the love of the Father motivates you to serve Him and love others. Those two things become more important than anything else. You can't proclaim your trust in God if you haven't worked this issue out. Where's your heart?

God's Word

The unfolding of your words gives light;
it gives understanding to the simple.
Psalm 119:130

It is difficult to trust someone you don't really know. As our relationship with God grows we learn to trust Him more. How do we establish this relationship? It can only be established by knowing God. We learn to know Him by reading His Word.

God speaks to us through His Word, revealing His character, His love for us, and His direction for our lives. So, it only makes sense that for our trust in God to grow deeper, we must spend time in His Word, finding His guidance and direction and understanding His love.

Let Go!

"For nothing is impossible with God."
Luke 1:37

Did you get that? Read that verse again ... and again. Nothing, absolutely nothing is impossible when God is involved. So, what's the issue with trusting Him? Do you question whether He loves you? His Word is filled, cover to cover, with His declarations of love. He shows you His love in a multitude of ways every single day. Do you fear that some things may simply be too big for Him? Some challenges may be too hard for Him to handle? Read the verse again – *nothing* is impossible with God.

The issue of trusting Him is more that He might not do things the way you want them done, right? Well, He may not. But He sees a bigger picture than you do. So, let go and trust Him – remember, He can handle whatever comes up. Nothing is impossible with Him.

Sticking Together

*I long to see you so that I may impart
to you some spiritual gift to make you
strong – that is, that you and I may be
mutually encouraged by each other's faith.*
Romans 1:11-12

Life is not meant to be lived alone. God is pleased when we live in community – with friends and family. One reason for this is that we can encourage one another. Trusting is not easy when the tough times seem to go on and on. Friends and family can encourage you to hang in there. When your own faith is stretched to the limit, a friend's faith can hold you up until you get back on your spiritual feet.

When two people trust together, walking side by side, their faith is twice as strong. Don't try to go it alone. Let others encourage you.

Short-Term Winners

Do not fret because of evil men or be
envious of those who do wrong; for like
the grass they will soon wither, like
green plants they will soon die away.

Psalm 37:1-2

Does it sometimes seem as if the bad guys are winning? When you look around at the condition of our world and see wars, poverty, abused children, the rich getting richer while the poor get poorer, prejudice, oppression ... and on and on, do you wonder where God is?

This verse reminds us to keep trusting in God, because the bad guys will get their due one day and God will prevail! Put your trust in God, because what He has to offer – the hope of heaven – is the only thing that's going to stick around. The "winners" on earth will be the losers in eternity, if they don't put their trust in God.

Not Alone

"But the Counselor, the Holy Spirit,
whom the Father will send in my
name, will teach you all things and will
remind you of everything I have said."
John 14:26

We're not alone. There's comfort in knowing that, isn't there? The process of understanding God and learning to trust Him is not something we have to tackle alone. He sent the Holy Spirit to teach us and remind us of everything Jesus said. We are not alone in the struggles of life. The Holy Spirit indwells all believers and works to help us become more like Christ by teaching us about Him.

How does this help with trusting God? We have a personal advocate helping us understand the Father and who helps us pray when we can't find the words to say. The Spirit's presence is another evidence of God's incredible love and concern for us.

Powerful God

Ah, Sovereign LORD, you have made the heavens and the earth by your great power and outstretched arm. Nothing is too hard for you.
Jeremiah 32:17

What would it take for you to stop trying to control your own life and just let God have it? What would it take for you to trust Him? God made everything there is, from a delicate flower to a powerful volcano. He made the ant and the humpback whale. God made seasons, thunderstorms, sunsets ... and you. He gave you a mind and heart. He gave you free will and a conscience. He knows all about you and how complicated your thoughts are and what your decision-making process is like. He knows it all ... and He loves you.

Ever-Present Love

Test me, O LORD, and try me, examine my heart and my mind; for your love is ever before me, and I walk continually in your truth.
Psalm 26:2-3

God's love is always before you. You can trust God to examine your heart and mind; to know the deep dark secrets that you don't let any other person know about because He won't walk away. You can trust Him to know what you're really, truly like and not throw up His hands in disgust and walk away.

He loves you. He looks deep into your heart and sees if your desire is to walk in His truth, even if you repeatedly stumble and fall. He will pick you up and help you to try again because when He looks at you, His eyes are continually filled with love.

Magnificent Love

*"For God so loved the world that he gave
his one and only Son, that whoever believes
in him shall not perish but have eternal life."*

John 3:16

How could you not trust someone who loves you
this much? God wanted a relationship with you so
badly that He made a way to bridge the gap of sin
between you and Him. He willingly allowed His
only Son to come to earth, be persecuted, suffer and
die ... for your sins. He didn't have any, so when
He paid that ultimate price, it was for you and me.
Then God raised Him back to life and brought Him
back to heaven to live with Him.

He worked out this elaborate plan because He
loves you and wants a relationship with you. When
you stop and think about it ... well, God is
definitely worthy of your trust, right?

Remember Christ

Therefore, since Christ suffered in his body,
arm yourselves also with the same attitude,
because he who has suffered in his body is
done with sin. As a result, he does not live
the rest of his earthly life for evil human
desires, but rather for the will of God.
1 Peter 4:1-2

The way you live shows what you really think of God. You can use Christian words, pray, tithe, even teach Sunday school, but how you treat your co-workers, your honesty, integrity, and concern for others, how you spend your spare time, what's important to you ... those are the things that show what you really think of God.

You are to have a Christlike attitude and hold firm to your faith in Him. He didn't live for the praise of people, but desired to do the will of God. Follow Christ's example – trust God to be your strength.

Stay Focused

*Look to the LORD and his
strength; seek his face always.*
Psalm 105:4

You won't be able to trust God fully if you don't stay focused on Him. Keep your eyes on the Lord. What does that mean? Don't let your mind and heart get sidetracked from what is truly important. Life is filled with temptations to put your trust in other people or in things like money or recognition. These will only lead to disappointment and failure.

Keep your eyes firmly focused on Jesus, seeking His guidance and direction daily, seeking to become more and more like Him in your attitudes and behavior. The better you become at keeping your eyes on His face the more your trust in Him will grow.

Healthy Trust

Whoever trusts in his riches will fall,
but the righteous will thrive like a green leaf.
Proverbs 11:28

This verse says it all, doesn't it? Those who depend on their money to get them through life are doomed. If you think your wealth is what gives you worth and value, you are sadly mistaken. Your wealth can buy you out of some situations, but it can't buy your way into heaven. If you respect others because of their status or their wealth, shame on you. A person with money is not necessarily a better person than someone who is poor.

Your trust should be placed in God and in your walk with Him. He will help you make right choices. He will help you grow in love and concern for others. When your trust is correctly placed, you will thrive and grow like a healthy plant.

Unfailing Love

Many are the woes of the wicked,
but the LORD's unfailing love
surrounds the man who trusts in him.
Psalm 32:10

Unconditional love ... love that never fails. Now that's something you can sink your trust into. Perhaps you've had experience with human love. It can be good, strong, compelling – but not perfect. Sometimes people we love disappoint us, sometimes they break our trust. But God's love is unfailing. When you trust Him, His love will surround you, and it never fails.

Trusting God means being honest with Him, telling Him about your concerns, your fears and your problems. You don't have to fear telling Him anything because nothing you say will make Him withdraw His love. His love is unfailing. It is constant. Trust it.

A Good Fragrance

Thanks be to God, who always leads us in triumphal procession in Christ and through us spreads everywhere the fragrance of the knowledge of him. For we are to God the aroma of Christ among those who are being saved and those who are perishing.

2 Corinthians 2:14-15

What an incredible reason to place your day in, day out trust in God. By trusting Him to direct your paths and guide your thoughts, you have the opportunity to be used by Him. Imagine being known as a person who leaves the fragrance of God everywhere she goes. Others will know that God has been in your midst by the fragrance you leave behind.

God will use you to be the aroma of Christ both to the saved and the unsaved. God will lead you in this process. All you have to do is be available to Him and trust Him to lead you.

Happy Trust

*Surely this is our God; we trusted in him, and
he saved us. This is the LORD, we trusted
in him; let us rejoice and be glad in his salvation.*

Isaiah 25:9

Trust is simple and yet it isn't. Your trust is going
to land somewhere. When a person recognizes her
need for salvation, because of her own sinfulness,
and that salvation can only come from God, then
it only makes sense to place her trust in God.
However, Satan is going to fight that decision every
moment of every day. So, trusting God is not a one
time decision.

Every morning you decide anew to trust God
because He has saved you. You decide each day to
be glad in Him. Some days you may have to make
that decision many times, but it is a decision that
will always be worth it.

SEPTEMBER

The Joy of Marriage

Soft and Gentle

A gentle answer turns away wrath,
but a harsh word stirs up anger.

Proverbs 15:1

Honesty time ... do you sometimes feel that your husband just doesn't have a clue? You can talk until you're blue in the face, but he just never seems to "get it". Finally, in desperation you may raise your voice (you know ... just a little). Then he gets all huffy and well, things just go downhill from there.

Well, the secret to stopping that downward spiral is right here – don't do the voice-raising thing. When you let a harsh word slip out, it's going to bring retaliation from your partner and no good is going to come from that. When you're about to lose your cool, stop; count to ten; speak gently. You'll be glad that you did.

Kindness Is as Kindness Does

"Be merciful, just as your Father is merciful."
Luke 6:36

Marriage is hard work sometimes. Blending two people and two styles of living into one is bound to hit some rough spots. If that seems to be happening a lot in your marriage, stop and think about this: Think about what made you fall for this guy in the first place. Something attracted you to him and caused love to grow. Remember that he is a genuinely nice guy and he really isn't trying to irritate you (come on, admit this).

Now, "cut him some slack" and be kind to him ... because the truth is God is granting you that same kind of mercy. Everyone messes up sometimes. Respond to your husband's mistakes with mercy and with love – just as God responds to yours.

A Love Goal

Love never fails.
1 Corinthians 13:8

What an amazing statement that is ... love never fails. Everything else in life will fall away. Careers will end, children will grow up and move away, the "things" of life may rust and decay, friends may disappoint ... but love never fails. It's the one thing you can count on. God's love for you is constant and sure and it never disappoints. It's the one thing that will be left standing at the end of the day. It's the standard.

Let that love be the guide for your love for your spouse. Make your unfailing love for him a giving and forgiving love; a love that puts his needs first, a love that doesn't ask for anything in return; a love that never fails.

Fret Not!

Refrain from anger and turn from wrath;
do not fret – it leads only to evil.
Psalm 37:8

Are you a "fretter"? Do you latch on to something your husband says (or doesn't say) or pick up a curious tone in his voice and fret over it? Do you create scenarios in your mind as to what might develop or what he might be thinking? How much mental energy do you spend imagining scenes that your husband knows nothing about? And then all he has to say is one wrong word and *boom* – it's explosion time!

Fretting leads to evil, which is why the psalmist says not to do it. He put that bit of wisdom together with staying away from anger. Keep the lines of communication open and don't fret your way through one-sided mental conversations; that will only lead to trouble.

Teamwork!

*Let us consider how we may spur one
another on toward love and good deeds.*
Hebrews 10:24

No man is an island – and neither is any woman – especially if you're married. When God created mankind, He intended for us to function as a community that lives and works together. When He brings two people together as husband and wife, they can best show their mutual love by helping each other become the best people they can be.

Spend some time praying about (and thinking about) how you can spur your husband on toward love and good deeds. Be specific and obvious in that encouragement. Remember to speak and act in ways he understands. As he grows in those acts of love and good deeds, he will become a better, deeper person and just may begin encouraging you in the same ways! What a team!

CAROLYN LARSEN

SEPTEMBER 6

The Dreaded Word

Wives, submit to your husbands as to the Lord.
Ephesians 5:22

Does this verse make the hair on your neck stand up? In these days of equality and liberation, submitting to your husband is not a popular topic. Calm down, maybe it's not as bad as you think. There is a foundation that is often overlooked – your husband loves you and wants the best for you and your marriage. Together you are seeking to be examples of God's love to those around you, especially your children.

Submitting means not insisting on your own way, building him up and supporting him, especially in front of others, deferring to his wisdom and intelligence on matters where he knows more than you do. Working as a team to make your home, your marriage, your ministry the best it can be.

Reality Check

*She brings him good, not
harm, all the days of her life.*
Proverbs 31:12

Life gets busy, doesn't it? Most women feel like they meet themselves coming and going. Between keeping up with the housework, a job, driving kids around, school committees, church committees ... well, there just aren't enough hours in the day. One thing that can suffer most in all the busyness, is your relationship with your husband. How many evenings is he at home with the kids while you're out being busy? At the end of the day, do you have energy left for conversation, let alone intimacy?

This is a gentle reminder to keep your priorities straight. Give your marriage relationship the time it deserves. Give your husband the time and energy he deserves. Bring good to him by showing him how important he is to you.

Cold Nights

If two lie down together, they will keep
warm. But how can one keep warm alone?
Ecclesiastes 4:11

Have you ever been really cold and experienced the warmth of someone's arm around your shoulder? Have you ever been afraid or worried and appreciated the comfort of having another person beside you? Look at this verse as a reminder that you and your husband should stick together because in the ups and downs of life, you will both get mighty cold if you're alone.

Even the good times will be more pleasant as you share them with one another, building memories and adding depth to your relationship. And the hard times will not be so lonely or frightening if you are together, emotionally and spiritually. Don't be afraid to need one another.

Love Always

Do everything in love.
1 Corinthians 16:14

What's your motivation? Think back to when you first fell in love with Mr. Wonderful. Remember how you couldn't do enough for him? Perhaps you baked cookies, ran errands, sent little love notes – anything you could think of to show him how much you cared. What about now? Can you honestly say that love is constantly evident in the words you speak, things you do, choices you make, priorities you live out?

Doing everything in love means putting others' needs and desires ahead of your own, it means giving, sharing, encouraging and sacrificing yourself in those actions. Think about this in relation to your spouse. Doing everything in love means not having any hidden agendas, or selfish goals. It means your thoughts, words, deeds are all motivated by love … always.

True Forgiveness

Bear with each other and forgive whatever grievances you may have against one another. Forgive as the Lord forgave you.

Colossians 3:13

Do you keep a mental ledger of your spouse's mistakes, bad choices or slights toward you? Maybe you're pretty good at outwardly keeping your cool, perhaps you're even proud of how forgiving you appear to be. But you just quietly store up your complaints and hurts until you reach bursting point. Then the explosion comes as a total surprise to your spouse.

A relationship built on this kind of interaction will not grow stronger. A better plan is to forgive ... really forgive your spouse, whether his actions are intentional or unintentional. Remember that God forgives you moment by moment. Extend that same generous, loving forgiveness to your spouse.

Think Before Speaking

Reckless words pierce like a sword,
but the tongue of the wise brings healing.
Proverbs 12:18

Words, words, words. Words can encourage, cheer and lift a person's self-esteem. Words can express love, hope and joy. Words spoken wisely and gently can build trust in a relationship. The opposite is also true. Words that tumble from your mouth without thought or consideration as to how they will affect the heart of those who hear them can do great damage. They can pierce your self-esteem, heart and even hope. It's so easy in a marriage to let reckless words shoot from spouse to spouse. We are sometimes inconsiderate in how we treat our spouses.

This verse is a powerful reminder that wise words bring healing while reckless words bring pain. Think before speaking. Pray for wisdom and control to speak wisely and kindly.

Advantage Love

Knowledge puffs up, but love builds up.
1 Corinthians 8:1

Do you enjoy being around a person who thinks he knows everything about everything? People who always have to be first; always have to be right; and always must have the last word are not easy to be friends with ... or married to. Love, on the other hand, builds others up. It encourages others to speak their minds and share their opinions. How does that work in your marriage? It means listening to your husband's ideas and opinions and not insisting that your way is always right or belittling his ideas and comments.

Love looks for ways to help your husband feel intelligent and useful. Love will build him up so that he's more and more confident and grows in wisdom. Your husband, your marriage and you will benefit from living in love.

Money-Loving

For the love of money is a root of all kinds of evil.
1 Timothy 6:10

How many marriages break up because of arguments over money? Each of us is a product of our upbringing and we come into marriage with preconceived notions as to who will manage the money and how it will be spent. In the early years when money is often tight, arguments about money abound. It is so important to have a good attitude about money. Getting more money should never become more important than the people in your life.

Loving and pursuing money can make the people you love feel less important to you than your career or the bank account you watch so closely. If money is important to you, step back and look at the whole picture. Is the love of money damaging your marriage? If so, this is your wake-up call to do something about it.

Count To Ten

Everyone should be quick to listen,
slow to speak, and slow to become angry.
James 1:19

This is a good measuring stick for communication. But do you find yourself sometimes living in reverse to this verse – slow to listen, quick to speak, and quick to become angry? Yes, it is easy to slip into such behavior. But think about how damaging it is to a relationship.

God created us to live in community with one another ... especially in marriage. You and your husband are a team with the goal of moving and thinking in unity with one another. If you are slow to listen you'll be spouting off or exploding at him without ever really hearing what he has to say. That stifles communication. Remember the old adage ... count to ten before speaking and make quick listening a priority.

A Matter of Trust

A gossip betrays a confidence,
but a trustworthy man keeps a secret.
Proverbs 11:13

It's all about trust. For your relationship with your husband to grow deeper in intimacy you must be able to trust one another. He has to know that whatever he tells you will not go any farther than your ears. He has to believe that his thoughts and feelings, which are meant only for you, will not be shared with your best friend – even as a supposed matter of prayer.

Prayer is good, best friends are wonderful, but the depth of intimacy in the marriage relationship is special and must be guarded. You and your husband are a team and you must guard that special relationship by not revealing his confidences through a lazy comment, a humorous jab or flat out spilling the beans. Show your husband that he can trust you completely.

A Humble Example

*Clothe yourselves with humility toward
one another, because, "God opposes
the proud but gives grace to the humble."*
1 Peter 5:5

Christ left the glory of heaven to come to earth ... as a servant. He set quite an example for us to put the needs of others before our own wants and desires. Living in humility is an act of love. It shows true concern for the feelings and needs of those around you.

Do you emulate Christ's example in your home? Do you clothe yourself with humility – even when you're tired and stressed – that's when the rubber meets the road, isn't it? Ask God to help you empty yourself of ... you ... and fill your heart with the desire to live humbly toward those around you. You will be an example of Christ's incredible love to them.

A Woman's Work Is Never Done

She watches over the affairs of her
household and does not eat the bread of idleness.
Proverbs 31:27

This Proverbs 31 woman didn't sit around watching soap operas and eating bonbons. She didn't spend afternoons chatting over coffee with her friends. She made the work of keeping her home running smoothly a priority. These days many women work outside the home and come home in the evening to their household work so it's hard to imagine having any time for idleness.

Managing the home is a responsibility that women handle well because we multi-task well. It doesn't mean that we work all day at our jobs, then come home and work all night ... the responsibilities of the household can certainly be shared. But if your habit is to flip on the TV and crash or spend your time in some other unproductive way, it may be time to reprioritize.

R-e-s-p-e-c-t

Each one of you also must love his wife as he loves himself and the wife must respect her husband.
Ephesians 5:33

Have you ever been with your friends when someone tells a "My silly husband story"? That starts the ball rolling and before long husband stories are flying around the room. Most of us are guilty of such behavior – it's entertaining and sometimes it relieves a bit of the relationship stress. However, each time you tell a story about what your husband does or doesn't do, or how he doesn't have a clue about some things, you're breaking the command in this verse ... in public!

Making him the brunt of your humor does *not* show him respect. So, the next time a story or quick comment about your husband comes to mind, stop and think, "Will these words show respect to my husband?" If they don't – be quiet!

Sweet, Sweet Spirit

Do everything without complaining or arguing.
Philippians 2:14

"Honey, the toilet paper's gone." "The dog threw up." "Where's my black socks?" "Is my white shirt ironed?" Do those things sound familiar to you? Are you supposed to have the answer for everything – the be-all, know-all governor in your home? How do you handle that responsibility? Are you able to answer your husband's questions or comments without complaining or arguing? Sometimes you may feel that the weight of the household is on your shoulders, and maybe it is. But complaining and arguing won't help the situation. A gentle conversation that conveys how you feel is a better idea.

A sweet spirit accomplishes a lot more than an argumentative one. Be aware that you can build up your relationship or tear it down by the attitude you choose to have.

Paybacks

*Make sure that nobody pays back wrong
for wrong, but always try to be
kind to each other and to everyone else.*
1 Thessalonians 5:15

He didn't help with the housework, so you "forget" to iron his shirt. He didn't remember your anniversary, so you withhold sex. He made an unkind comment, so you stop talking altogether. Paybacks. "If you don't do this, I won't do that." Whew! Can you see how that will cause a relationship to spiral downward? Paybacks are relationship killers. If you find yourself in this kind of behavior ... stop.

When you have a problem with your spouse's behavior or comments, wouldn't it be better to talk with him about it rather than starting the payback cycle? He may not even realize that what he did sparked your payback behavior. It would be kinder and more loving to talk to him about it ... gently.

Community

*The Lord God said, "It is not good for the man
to be alone, I will make a helper suitable for him."*
Genesis 2:18

This is a wonderful verse because it shows us God's desire for us to live in relationships with one another. Helper doesn't mean servant, it doesn't imply a lesser being than the original creation. God saw that by himself man was incomplete, he needed a being like himself with whom he could share life.

Think about that term, "sharing". The relationship that's possible between a husband and wife is amazing – being best friends, sharing hopes, dreams, fears and worries, building each other up to be the best man and woman possible, serving God side by side, and on and on. God established community right here so that you could know that you are never alone in this world. Your spouse is your partner. Wonderful feeling!

Love

*Love is patient, love is kind. It does not
envy, it does not boast, it is not proud.
It is not rude, it is not self-seeking, it is not
easily angered, it keeps no record of wrongs.*
1 Corinthians 13:4-5

Remember when you "fell in love" with your sweetie. The sun rose and set on him. All your thoughts involved him. The prospect of establishing a home together made your heart flutter. Then you got married and perhaps the stars in your eyes faded. The fact is that sometimes it's hard to blend two lives and live together day in and day out. Our love gets more self-focused than it should.

The definition of love in this verse takes the focus off self. True love is servant love that lifts others up and is not self-motivated. What an incredible way to be loved ... and to love. It's possible – with God's help.

Three-Strand Strength

Though one may be overpowered,
two can defend themselves. A cord
of three strands is not quickly broken.
Ecclesiastes 4:12

God created us to live in community. We're not meant to try to make it on our own. Life is better when it is shared with someone. When the challenges of life knock you down, it's harder to pull yourself up if you're alone. You need someone telling you that you're not alone and that you can do what you need to do. Your husband can be the one who encourages you, helps you stand and even holds you accountable to make good choices.

The third strand mentioned in this verse is the Lord. He is the strand of steel, the strand that wraps around the other two and holds them tightly together. Don't forget to daily invoke His presence in your marriage relationship.

Joy

A cheerful look brings joy to the heart,
and good news gives health to the bones.
Proverbs 15:30

Whether you like it or not, the truth is that the woman often sets the atmosphere in the home. Women are so relational that husbands and children learn to watch the wife/mother to see how she is handling life and reacting to problems. This can seem to be unnecessary pressure – or, it can be viewed as an opportunity to set a tone of joy, trust and hope. It's a chance to demonstrate the faith you claim to have on the inside – in other words, a chance to put your money where your mouth is.

That doesn't mean forced or fake cheerfulness. It does mean trusting God, looking for signs of His work in your life, and sharing the joy you find in the relationships you share.

Self-Sacrificing Love

*This is how we know what love is: Jesus Christ
laid down his life for us. And we ought
to lay down our lives for our brothers.*

1 John 3:16

Jesus set quite an example for us of love that gives and gives, holding nothing back. He made those around Him the focus of His life. Now, we're told to live the same way. What does that mean in a marriage relationship? It means giving of your time and energy ... even when you don't feel like it.

The love Jesus modeled for us denies self by putting others first. It means thinking of what your partner might enjoy or prefer before you automatically do things your way. What kinds of things? How to spend free time, movie choices, dinner menus, even divisions of household chores. Lay down your life for your spouse and show real love to those around you.

Being There for Him

Encourage one another daily.
Hebrews 3:13

You see your husband every day. Hopefully you talk every evening about how the day has gone, what the high points and low points were for each of you. A husband and wife have the unique opportunity to encourage one another every single day. They have the chance to say, "You can do it. I know you can!" or "Hang in there, it will get better" or "No matter what happens, remember that I'm here for you when you come home."

Encouragement is the oxygen that keeps us running through the challenges life presents. Listen to one another so you learn the things that encourage one another. Then take the time and energy to do those things. Encourage one another every day.

Honesty Is the Best Policy

Do not lie to each other.
Colossians 3:9

Hiding charge card bills. Saying you went to work when you really went shopping with a friend. "Oh, honey, this dress only cost $75.00" (as you hide the $150 price tag). "No, I don't mind if you go to the game," (spoken through gritted teeth). Lying … from little white lies to great big bright red ones … will only hurt a relationship. Once you've been caught in a lie, it will be difficult for your spouse to trust you again.

Lying damages a relationship for a very long time. You will have to prove yourself over and over to reestablish trust once it has been broken. Don't take the chance – honesty is always the best policy and your relationship with your husband deserves the best.

Making the Break

For this reason a man will leave his father and mother and be united to his wife, and the two will become one flesh.
Ephesians 5:31

"A son is a son 'til he takes a wife, but a daughter's a daughter the rest of her life." Have you heard this before? It's saying that when a couple marries, the wife's relationship with her parents stays stronger than the husband's does. Not really fair.

But the truth of this verse is that when you marry, you establish a new loyalty and your responsibility is to one another above your parents. Never put your parents' opinions above your spouse ... learn from their wisdom ... but make decisions as husband and wife. And, above all ... never run home to momma instead of working out your problems with your husband.

Pray Continually

Pray continually.
1 Thessalonians 5:17

There are so many elements of a good marriage, so many things to think about as your love grows and your relationship develops. But the best thing you can do for your marriage is pray. Pray for your husband, asking God to guide and direct him. Ask God to give him wisdom and discernment. Pray for his spiritual growth and for God's blessings on his life.

Pray for your marriage to grow more and more intimate, for your relationship to grow deeper and deeper. Pray together. Pray for the concerns that you share. Pray for strength to withstand temptations. Pray for God's guidance and instruction in your marriage relationship. Ask God to use you as His servants, to minister and witness to His love. Never stop praying.

First Things First

Worship the LORD in the splendor of his holiness.
1 Chronicles 16:29

As you and your husband blend your two lives into one and work on growing your marriage stronger and stronger, this verse is very important. It reminds you not to forget that you have your own personal walk with Christ to keep vital and strong, too. Don't neglect your personal Bible study and prayer life. The best thing you can bring to your marriage is a strong walk with the Lord.

Even though you spend time praying with your husband and sharing a devotional time, don't think that couple time can replace your personal relationship with Christ. Continue to personally worship Him and be awed by His holiness.

OCTOBER

You Are Special

Working in Your Strength

It was he who gave some to be apostles,
some to be prophets, some to be evangelists,
and some to be pastors and teachers,
to prepare God's people for works of service,
so that the body of Christ may be built up.
Ephesians 4:11-12

Do you sometimes look around at other women and think, "What an amazing person she is?" Do you compare yourself to others and, in your own mind, come up short in the talent/ability department? You shouldn't. God has given you a purpose on this earth. He put you here for a reason.

Spend some time thinking about what you're good at. What do you get excited about doing? How can that interest relate to other people – building friendships or opportunities for encouragement? Begin working on your strengths and ask God to grow your abilities and to use you in works of service.

Formed By the Master

*"Before I formed you in the womb I knew
you, before you were born I set you apart;
I appointed you as a prophet to the nations."*
Jeremiah 1:5

God spoke these words to the prophet, Jeremiah, but they hold a powerful message for us, too. God knew each of us before we even began to grow in the womb. He set each of us aside for a specific life plan.

We're not here by accident. God doesn't waste energy with any action. He didn't create some people with specific gifts to do His work, but make the rest of us "extras" in the movie called life. He loves each of us and gave each of us abilities and talents. We each have the imprint of His hand on our lives.

Wonderful Works

*For you created my inmost being; you knit
me together in my mother's womb. I praise you
because I am fearfully and wonderfully made;
your works are wonderful, I know that full well.*
Psalm 139:13-14

God created the whole universe by simply speaking a word. He created the massive oceans, mountains, and deserts. He formed the lovely butterfly and the incredible sperm whale. He imagined flowers of thousands of forms and colors, and gigantic redwood trees. He is incredibly creative and powerful. And He made you.

A popular saying of years gone by is "God don't make junk." Believe that. God doesn't waste anything. He made you and His works are wonderful. If other people are tearing you down, ignore them. Believe in your own self-worth. God does.

Not By Your Own Hand

*For who makes you different from
anyone else? What do you have that you
did not receive? And if you did receive it,
why do you boast as though you did not?*

1 Corinthians 4:7

You are different from anyone else on this earth.
What do you consider your strengths – the things
you're really good at? Are you kind of proud of
those things? Do you sometimes look around at
others and in your mind do a little comparison …
to see where you come out on top? Why? Nothing
you have, nothing you are is of your own doing.

You have received every talent, every gift, every
success – from God. So, you've nothing to boast
about. You have only to thank Him for His work
in your life and His gifts to you. No
boasting. No pride. Just confidence.
And thankfulness.

Inner Being

*The LORD said to Samuel, "Do not consider
his appearance or his height, for I have
rejected him. The LORD does not look at the
things man looks at. Man looks at the outward
appearance, but the LORD looks at the heart."*
1 Samuel 16:7

People form impressions based on others' appearance. We put a lot of stock in outward appearance. Those who are pretty, well-dressed, slender, "put together" tend to get our immediate respect and honor. But those who don't grab our attention, but may have so much more to offer from the inside, are pushed aside.

Well, God doesn't do that. He looks at the heart and sees what our motives are, how much we care about obeying God, whether we care about others. So, that's the part of your being to work on. Be confident in the person you are on the inside – that's what really matters.

A Beautiful Spirit

*Your beauty should not come from outward
adornment, such as braided hair and the
wearing of gold jewelry and fine clothes.
Instead, it should be that of your inner self,
the unfading beauty of a gentle and quiet spirit,
which is of great worth in God's sight.*

1 Peter 3:3-4

Millions of dollars are spent by women each year
on beauty products and treatments, clothing and
jewelry. We want to look good. We care about our
outward appearance. Now, there's nothing wrong
with looking good and taking care of your body.
But be careful not to put too much importance on
that.

Your real beauty comes from inside – a kind and
gentle spirit and a heart that desires to serve and
honor God. Put your trust in God, rest in Him and
your peaceful, loving spirit will shine through.

Treasures!

For you are a people holy to the Lord your God. The Lord your God has chosen you out of all the peoples on the face of the earth to be his people, his treasured possession.

Deuteronomy 7:6

Wow! What does this verse do for your self-image? Even if you're in the slough of despair – thinking the most negative thoughts about yourself – this verse has to lift you up. You are among God's chosen people! You're part of His family, separated out of all the peoples on the earth.

The most amazing part of this verse is that you are His treasured possession. You must have something that you greatly treasure. You put it in a special place, handle it carefully … take good care of it. You are God's treasured possession. Ask God to open your eyes to how special you are to Him and how uniquely He made you.

Growing a Better World

Accept one another, then, just as Christ accepted you, in order to bring praise to God.
Romans 15:7

Jesus accepts us in all our imperfections, selfishness and all. He loves us. Knowing that He loves us, no matter what, should give us confidence. It helps us have a better attitude about life when we know we matter to someone. It's incredibly special when that someone is Jesus Christ.

That confidence gives us the ability and sensitivity to accept others in the same way. Acceptance begets confidence which begets kindness which begets acceptance. That will form better people, better servants, and a better world where Christ's love can be shared. Recognize Christ's acceptance of you and pass it on.

A Great Plan

*For we are God's workmanship, created in
Christ Jesus to do good works, which
God prepared in advance for us to do.*
Ephesians 2:10

What is your favorite thing that God created? Sunsets in Hawaii? Magnificent snowcapped mountains? The massive beautiful oceans teeming with life? Delicate roses? Soft, cuddly puppies? Whatever your favorite thing in creation is, you do recognize that it was made by God's hand, right? God's work of creation is amazing. He made incredibly complicated things and things that are simple in their beauty.

You are God's workmanship. He made you and not only did He make you, He also has a job for you to do. As He formed you, He planned what good works you could do for Him. You're not here by accident. You're not in the job you have or the relationships you enjoy by accident. God has a plan. Look for it.

No Surprises

*When I was woven together in the depths
of the earth, your eyes saw my unformed body.
All the days ordained for me were written
in your book before one of them came to be.*
Psalm 139:15-16

Nothing surprises God. He knew all about you before you made your appearance on this earth ... in fact He planned your debut. He decided what color eyes you would have, how tall you would grow. He had a hand in the choices you made to become who you are. While you toddled around the house at two years old, He looked into the future and saw the plans He had already laid out for you.

Nothing surprises Him, He knows the beginning from the end. So, don't forget to talk to Him about the big choices you have to make ... in fact, consult Him about every single choice.

He cares.

The Lighted Path

*"I am the light of the world. Whoever
follows me will never walk in darkness,
but will have the light of life."*
John 8:12

Do you sometimes feel like you're muddling through in darkness? You're not sure if you're on the right path, or even on any path? Well, there's one way to clear up those questions – follow Jesus. He's the only one who can illuminate the dark places in your heart.

By making a conscious effort to follow Him every day, you will be able to have the confidence that your steps are never in darkness. Even if you can't see the path ahead of you, you can trust that as you step out, the path will be lit, because He gives the light of life. He promises that you won't be in darkness ever again. Just follow Him.

Fearing God

Charm is deceptive, and beauty is fleeting;
but a woman who fears the Lord is to be praised.
Proverbs 31:30

This chapter of Proverbs often inspires guilt (and sometimes secret anger) in the hearts of women. This woman did it all! She was a good business woman, domestic goddess, and mother of the year all rolled into one. Of course, don't miss the little note in verse 15 that she did have servant girls. Some writers say that the woman described in this chapter is actually the best of several women all rolled together into one description.

Whatever the case, the characteristic described in verse 30 is definitely the most important thing said about this woman. She feared the Lord. She gave Him the honor and respect that was due Him. That's more praiseworthy than any of the other things said about her. Respect God and give Him the honor He deserves.

Finish Strong

I have fought the good fight, I have finished the race, I have kept the faith. Now there is in store for me the crown of righteousness, which the Lord, the righteous judge, will award to me on that day – and not only to me, but also to all who have longed for his appearing.

2 Timothy 4:7-8

When you come to the end of life, wouldn't you love to be able to say things like this about the way you lived your life. You can, you know.

Paul made a choice to stay on the path – everything that happened to him and every opportunity that came along was viewed through the filter of how it fit in with his walk with Christ. He was true to his commitment to follow Christ and, as far as we know, he never wavered from that decision.

Good Use of Time

Teach us to number our days aright,
that we may gain a heart of wisdom.
Psalm 90:12

Your life should be lived so that you become more and more wise – with God's wisdom. Praying this prayer seeks God's direction in making good choices that will help you move forward in becoming the person God desires.

Each of us needs to seek God's wisdom in using our time wisely and being purposeful in reaching our full potential, in becoming Christlike and serving God with our whole being. That means that we will become more like Him so that those around us will see improvements in the way we treat others and in the choices we make. When God teaches us wisdom, we can be confident that He is working in our lives and is pleased with our service.

The Best Choice

*"What good will it be for a man if he gains
the whole world, yet forfeits his soul? Or what
can a man give in exchange for his soul?"*
Matthew 16:26

There is nothing in this world that is more important than our relationship with God. We spend so much time on the "stuff" of life, the stuff that the world has decided is important. Even as children of God we fall victim to the message that accumulating more and more money, having a bigger house, nicer car, sky-rocketing career, slimmer body, and all the other things the world says is important are, in fact, important.

But those things amount to nothing in the face of eternity. When you decide to focus your heart and mind on knowing and serving God, you've made the best choice.

A Focused Heart

*These [trials] have come so that your faith –
of greater worth than gold, which perishes
even though refined by fire – may be proved
genuine and may result in praise, glory
and honor when Jesus Christ is revealed.*

1 Peter 1:7

No one enjoys hard times. No one looks forward to painful experiences, but a greater good can come from the hurt and pain that life sometimes brings. The realization that God is working in your heart and growing a stronger, deeper faith can put your difficulties in perspective.

When your heart is focused on worshiping and serving God in every aspect of your life, then even though you don't celebrate pain, you can rejoice that God is working in your life, changing you and making you more like Him.

The Worthy Life

I urge you to live a life worthy of the calling
you have received. Be completely humble and
gentle; be patient, bearing with one another in love.
Ephesians 4:1-2

Sometimes women seem to struggle with knowing what God wants them to do with their lives; what they should be doing to serve Him. They have trouble "finding themselves." Living for God ... and just living in general ... is a process that unfolds and develops through the years.

However, there is no real reason to say that you don't know what God wants you to do. There are basic things that He has made very clear and they are good beginning points in living the Christian life: the way you relate to other people. The beginning of the worthy calling is to begin living in love with others.

All Cleaned Up

All have sinned and fall short of the glory of
God, and are justified freely by his grace through
the redemption that came by Christ Jesus.
Romans 3:23-24

So, you're not perfect – no one is. So you make mistakes – everyone does. Don't let yourself fall into the trap of looking around at others and thinking they have their lives all together and since you don't – you must be a failure. It just isn't so.

The Bible confirms that ALL of us are sinners. ALL of us fall short of God's glory. The hope that covers this depressing fact is that Jesus Christ paid the price for our sins. His death and resurrection cleaned us up and presents us to God as brand new. That's a fact. So don't get down on yourself for repeated failures and sins. Look at the hope of Christ's gift to you.

Set Apart

Know that the LORD has set apart the godly for himself; the LORD will hear when I call to him.

Psalm 4:3

Do you sometimes feel alone in the world, even though you're surrounded by people? Perhaps you feel that no one seems to really understand you. Or perhaps those around you are caught up in their own situations or pain and they can't give you what you need.

The psalmist understood that feeling. He also understood that his choice to seek God, his choice to follow God, meant he was set apart for God and that God would hear when he cried out to Him. Did you catch that – set apart for God. Set apart like a treasure, part of a special group. You are set apart for God because He loves you. He will hear when you call to Him.

The Best Love

We know and rely on the love God has for us. God is love. Whoever lives in love lives in God, and God in him.

1 John 4:16

It feels so good to know you are loved. When you believe that someone truly loves you, that nothing you thoughtlessly say or do can destroy that love, you can rest in it.

The truth is, the only One who completely loves you that way is God. He loves you unconditionally. He sees the best in you and the worst in you and loves you still. You can trust His love. There's a freedom in that, a freedom to explore and grow in your faith and know that, even if you stumble and fall, He won't walk away. He is love.

Thinking of Others

*"My command is this: Love each other as
I have loved you. Greater love has no one
than this, that he lay down his life for his friends."*
John 15:12-13

Getting your mind off your own problems can really help your attitude. Granted, it's not always easy to think about what's going on in someone else's life when you're stressed about your own – but doing so is one aspect of living out this verse.

Focusing on someone else, pushing your own wants and desires and problems aside to be sensitive to someone else is one way of laying down your life for a friend. This is serving God and obeying His commands. A side benefit is that you'll feel better about yourself!

A Healthy Outlook

A cheerful heart is good medicine,
but a crushed spirit dries up the bones.
Proverbs 17:22

Have you ever known someone who seems to have a perpetual black cloud floating above them? Someone who generally sees a glass as half empty instead of half full? Such people aren't much fun to be around, are they? When a person gets into a negative cycle, it's very hard to get out of. They begin to see the bad in every situation and can't find much to give them hope. Negativity breeds negativity.

Make the effort to find one thing to be happy or thankful about each day. In this way you will, day by day, climb the staircase that leads away from a crushed spirit. Rediscovering joy and thankfulness will renew your spirit and give you a healthier outlook on all of life.

Believe It!

*"Are not two sparrows sold for a penny? Yet not
one of them will fall to the ground apart from
the will of your Father. And even the very hairs
on your head are all numbered. So don't be afraid;
you are worth more than many sparrows."*
Matthew 10:29-31

When you cry out to God for help, but nothing happens, do you feel like you're on God's "B" list? Do you wonder if there are other people to whom He pays more attention – whose prayers are answered quickly and for whom decisions are clear? Do you feel that you get God's leftovers – whatever is left after dealing with the important people? Not so, my friend.

God knows how many hairs are on your head. He knows every bird that falls from the sky and you are worth far more to Him than they are. Believe it. He loves you.

Clean Up Your Life

*Those controlled by the sinful
nature cannot please God.*
Romans 8:8

Trying to please God without obeying Him is as useless as butting your head against a brick wall. The Scripture is clear that God is only pleased when we make every effort to live as a new person filled with His indwelling Spirit. If you're feeling bad about your spiritual walk and questioning why you don't seem to be growing any closer to God, take a serious look at your life. Things may look good from the outside, but you know the attitudes and motivations of your heart.

If you're still living as the old, sinful you, filled with selfishness and greed, even though no one except you and God know it, you are not pleasing Him. Clean up your life, then stand before God and see what He will do for you!

Pretty Packages

"The good man brings good things out of the good stored up in him, and the evil man brings evil things out of the evil stored up in him."
Matthew 12:35

Don't you feel special when you receive a beautifully wrapped gift with ornate ribbons and bows? However, things are not always as lovely on the inside as the outer packaging might suggest. It doesn't matter how pretty the paper or how fancy the ribbon if there is garbage inside.

The same is true of a life. You can seemingly have your life together, know the right things to say and do, but if there is not goodness in your heart, it will eventually become apparent. Don't waste time working on your packaging – spend time with God, confess your sin, seek to grow in Him, then the inner you will truly be beautiful and it will show through!

Relationship Busters

*A quick-tempered man does foolish
things, and a crafty man is hated.*
Proverbs 14:17

Quick tempers are like lightning bolts. They strike quickly, come from out of nowhere and often leave major damage behind them. A nasty temper flare-up can scar another person's self-esteem, damage a ministry, ruin relationships and leave you very lonely. Similarly, sly craftiness that attempts to manipulate others into doing what you want will cause others to mistrust you and dislike being in situations where they must work with you or even associate with you.

Both of these actions will damage relationships with others and service to God. Jesus said that loving God and loving others are the two greatest commandments. Keep your temper and your motivations under control in order to be the person God wants you to be.

Baby Steps

*Therefore, we do not lose heart. Though
outwardly we are wasting away, yet
inwardly we are being renewed day by day.*
2 Corinthians 4:16

How many times does a baby fall down on her way
to becoming a toddler? A child first pulls herself
to standing, then holds on to a table and scoots
around it. Then with eagerness and anticipation,
she steps away ... and falls. She gets up and starts
the whole process over again – falling down over
and over. But no child has ever given up and just
decided to stay on the floor and voluntarily crawl
through life.

We should have that same kind of perseverance
in our Christian walk. Don't lose heart because of
failures. Don't lose heart because of aging or illness
or discouragement or anything else. Remember
that God is teaching you and growing you into a
likeness of Himself.

Love, No Matter What

Above all, love each other deeply,
because love covers over a multitude of sins.
1 Peter 4:8

Have you ever baked a cake, gently placing the layers on the plate to frost and just as you lay the top layer on, it splits right down the middle? Frustrating, eh? But you cover up the problem by piling extra frosting over that crack and smoothing it in – then there is no evidence of the problem underneath. Love can do that. We all make mistakes in relationships. We behave selfishly; we say unkind or thoughtless things; we just mess up sometimes. What can cover over those relationship sins? Not arrogance or pride. Not money or gifts.

The only thing that really covers the problem is love. Love doesn't intentionally hurt someone, so when the hurt accidentally happens, the knowledge that love is present will help the healing begin.

OCTOBER 29

Patient Wisdom

A man's wisdom gives him patience;
it is to his glory to overlook an offense.
Proverbs 19:11

You don't have to point out every mistake that someone makes. Your patience in dealing with other people shows your wisdom. Others will notice if you keep a score sheet of who did what to whom and how many times. After a while they'll find reasons not to be around you. It's better to be patient with others, as you would like them to be with you.

This verse suggests that patience isn't an easy thing. That's why it is to your glory when it is shown. Ask God to help you be more patient ... with someone in particular? Ask Him to give you the strength to overlook things and to not even need to keep a score sheet. Then remember to thank Him for His patience with you!

Contentment

But godliness with contentment is great gain. For we brought nothing into this world, and we can take nothing out of it.
1 Timothy 6:6-7

Think of a picture of contentment – a baby who is freshly fed, burped, diapered and snuggled in Mother's arms. Contentment, peace, there is nothing more she needs at the moment. Do you have contentment in your life? Or are you constantly striving to have more stuff.

Godliness with contentment could simply mean an awareness that each new day is a gift from God. It could mean understanding that all you have is from His hand. That can relieve the pressure to work so hard and allows you to rest in Him and be grateful for whatever material possessions you have. Seek contentment from God as you move through your days.

Brave Courage

Be strong and courageous, and do the work.
Do not be afraid or discouraged,
for the LORD God, my God, is with you.
1 Chronicles 28:20

God is faithful. When He gives you a job to do, He will help you do it. He will not start you out, then half way through the project back away and say, "You're on your own!" There is no reason to be afraid or discouraged because if God is on your side, how could anything or anyone possibly hurt you?

The hardest part of this process is believing that God is truly present with you. Review how God has met your needs in life, draw strength from those memories coupled with this promise – God is with you. He will not let you go.

NOVEMBER

Loving Obedience

Single Job

Fear God and keep his commandments,
for this is the whole duty of man.
Ecclesiastes 12:13

The busyness of life is sometimes overwhelming. You can feel as if you're just checking one commitment off your list before going on to the next. Sometimes life is so busy that it's hard to find any meaning in life, even if the commitments keeping you busy are church or Christian commitments. That's when it's time to reassess your priorities.

The Bible says that the whole duty of man – the major work of man – is to fear (respect) God and keep His commandments. That means you must know His commandments and you must commit to living a life of obedience to Him. As you do so, you find meaning in your life by honoring and glorifying God in all you do.

Open-Book Life

We know that we have come to know him
if we obey his commands. The man who says,
"I know him," but does not do what he
commands is a liar, and the truth is not in him.
1 John 2:3-4

Don't gossip about others with one breath and proclaim that you are God's child with the next. If you choose to be disrespectful to others, don't try to witness to them later. Your actions speak louder than your words.

Proclaiming your faith in God but treating others badly shows that you haven't really given your heart to God. Obeying the basic commands given in Scripture is evidence that you take your relationship with Christ seriously enough to change your actions. Don't bother with the proclamations if your actions don't back them up.

New Heart

"I will give you a new heart and put a new spirit in you; I will remove from you your heart of stone and give you a heart of flesh. I will put my Spirit in you and move you to follow my decrees and be careful to keep my laws."
Ezekiel 36:26-27

"You can't teach an old dog new tricks." Maybe you feel that way about learning to obey God ... "It's too hard to change old habits. I'll never learn to obey God's commands." Well, the good news is that you don't have to do this on your own.

God promises that when you become His child, He will give you a new heart and the gift of His Spirit. The Spirit will help you learn to follow God's commands. You're not on your own!

Running Light

*Therefore, since we are surrounded by
such a great cloud of witnesses, let us throw
off everything that hinders and the sin
that so easily entangles, and let us run with
perseverance the race marked out for us.*
Hebrews 12:1

Have you noticed that runners wear the bare minimum of clothing? That makes it easier to run. If they ran wearing heavy winter coats and snow boots, they would quickly tire and not have a chance of winning the race.

The writer of Hebrews made a good analogy for us here. We're running the race of faith; a race that makes our faith deeper and our trust stronger as we run. So, we've got to get rid of the "junk" that can weigh us down. There are no secret sins. You can't keep a couple of favorite sins in the closet and think no one will know. God knows.

Learning To Obey

Jesus replied, "If anyone loves me,
he will obey my teaching. My Father
will love him, and we will come to
him and make our home with him."
John 14:23

Love and obedience cannot be separated. Jesus said this over and over ... loving leads to obeying. Think about people you love – you probably try to please them and do things you know will make them happy. It brings you joy to do things for them. The way you can bring joy to God is by obeying Him. What's the best way to know how to obey Him?

You have to spend time in His Word, gaining understanding of what it means to obey Him. Resolve before God to open your heart to Him and allow Him to reveal areas in your life that you need to work on. Let Him teach you.

Deliberate Sins

*If we deliberately keep on sinning after
we have received the knowledge of the truth,
no sacrifice for sins is left, but only a fearful
expectation of judgment and of raging fire
that will consume the enemies of God.*

Hebrews 10:26-27

A fool knows the right thing to do but doesn't do it.
When God's commandments become clear to you
and you understand the difference between right
and wrong, from God's perspective, you'd better
obey what you know to be right. If you continue to
live the way you've always lived and try to justify
your behavior, you're just fooling yourself.

Scripture is clear that deliberately continuing
to sin when you know better, is a slap in the face
to Christ's sacrificial death for your sins. You will
face judgment for your deliberate disobedience.
Don't sin ... obey.

School of Faith

*Teach me your way, O LORD, and I
will walk in your truth; give me an
undivided heart, that I may fear your name.*
Psalm 86:11

Your doctor probably has a diploma hanging on his wall signifying that he has completed the study program to qualify him to be a doctor. He has learned everything he needs to know to take care of you and your family. The school of faith is nothing like that. You will only graduate from learning to walk with God when you get to heaven. As long as you're on this earth, your education continues.

Thankfully, God will help you in your study program. He even gives you a private tutor – the Holy Spirit. The psalmist prayed for a heart that would be able to singularly focus on knowing God. That's a prayer we all should pray.

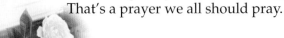

Rules of the Road

*I have hidden your word in my
heart that I might not sin against you.*
Psalm 119:11

When a teenager is preparing to take her driver's license test, she studies the Rules of the Road booklet religiously. She doesn't want to take any chance of failing the test. Her focus, her goal, is to know that information.

We should approach knowing God's Word with even more eagerness. God's Word is our Rules of the Road for life. In it, God reveals His guidelines for the way we live among each other and how we relate to Him. By knowing His Word so well that it is implanted in our hearts, we have a clear understanding of what actions are sinful. Know His Word ... it will help you learn obedience.

Get Rid of Sin

*"If your right hand causes you to sin,
cut it off and throw it away. It is better
for you to lose one part of your body
than for your whole body to go into hell."*
Matthew 5:30

Flip Wilson used to do a comic routine that always ended with the punch line, "The devil made me do it!" He used that little phrase to justify a myriad of bad behaviors. Justification ... do you try to justify the reasons for your sin? Do you make excuses as to why what you're doing is okay?

Jesus said that there is no justification. He said if anything makes you sin – get rid of it. Sin ... disobeying God ... is serious. Don't knowingly let anything stand in the way of obeying God.

Long Term

*The world and its desires pass away, but
the man who does the will of God lives forever.*
1 John 2:17

We invest so much time and energy in the things of
this world. We work at careers that we mistakenly
think make us more important and successful. We
buy bigger homes that take more time to care for. We
desire more gadgets, more vacations, more jewelry.
We care so much about the world's standards of
success.

The reality is that all those things will pass away.
They will not last. The one thing that will last is our
obedience to God. We go into eternity with that
one thing. It is all that lasts. Don't let the "stuff" of
this world get in the way of knowing and obeying
God. It's what really matters.

Hold Fast

*Be very careful to keep the commandment
and the law that Moses the servant of the
LORD gave you: to love the LORD your God,
to walk in all his ways, to obey his commands,
to hold fast to him and to serve him
with all your heart and all your soul.*

Joshua 22:5

A cross-country runner leads the race. She rounds the last bend with legs aching and lungs throbbing. The finish line is in sight. She knows that she has a good lead on her nearest competitor. Then, for no apparent reason, she stops running. The other runners pass by her and finish the race. Why would a competitor quit when the finish line was in sight?

This warning from Joshua encourages us to keep learning about and obeying God. Give it everything – all your heart and soul. Hold on to Him until the day you go to heaven.

Surface Appearances

If we claim to have fellowship with him yet walk
in the darkness, we lie and do not live by the truth.

1 John 1:6

"You can't judge a book by its cover." That expression holds true for many things in life, and Christianity is one of those things. A person can know all the "spiritual" things to say. She can be active in church, teaching, doing women's ministry or singing in the choir. She can *do* all the right things ... but if she isn't obeying God in her heart, she is a liar.

How does this work? Obeying God begins in the heart. If she has private sins and attitudes that are disobedient to God, then all the "works" in the world will not make her holy. Obeying begins in the heart. If you aren't obeying Him there, you'd better reevaluate where you stand.

Heart Occupant

Submit yourselves, then, to God. Resist the devil, and he will flee from you. Come near to God and he will come near to you.

James 4:7-8

Living in obedience to God is a daily battle. Satan doesn't want you to win even a minor victory, so you can never let your guard down. Submitting to God and resisting Satan means not struggling against the commands God has given. Don't argue – that's what Satan wants you to do. Don't try to justify your sins. That makes Satan smile, too.

Stay close to God on a daily basis, read His Word, pray, listen for His voice and He will come. He'll help you obey. He'll help you resist the temptations and tricks of Satan. Satan and God cannot occupy the same heart, so when God is there, Satan has to go.

Classroom Lessons

"I will instruct you and teach you in the way you should go; I will counsel you and watch over you."
Psalm 32:8

God Himself is your teacher. God's classroom is the world and His subject book is the Bible. You are an intern and He is teaching you. Lessons are learned through practical life situations. Your teacher is always with you to help you understand when you have learned a lesson and passed a test or not quite gotten the gist of a lesson and need to repeat a part of the course.

The guide book (the Bible) is always available to outline the lesson plans and give you practical help in learning the lessons. It's not easy to get an "A" in this class … it takes some work. But what an incredible privilege to be God's student.

Everyday Grind

He whose walk is upright fears the LORD,
but he whose ways are devious despises Him.
Proverbs 14:2

Everything you do in living your daily, everyday life –
everything – shows what your opinion of God is.
Scary thought, isn't it? Think about the way you
drive, your attitudes toward store clerks, responses
to telemarketers, how you handle the children, your
tone of voice when you speak to your husband,
what you think about a coworker ... everything
you think, say, and do in a given day.

If you respect and honor God, you will obey
Him and that will be evident in your daily life. A
big part of obeying God is loving others – all the
time. If your opinion of yourself is higher than your
opinion of God, that will show, too. Fear God ...
respect Him and obey Him.

Daily Battle

Live by the Spirit, and you will not gratify the desires of the sinful nature. For the sinful nature desires what is contrary to the Spirit, and the Spirit what is contrary to the sinful nature. They are in conflict with each other, so that you do not do what you want.

Galatians 5:16-17

Your heart is a battleground. The battle is whether you will obey God or satisfy the desires of your old sinful nature. Some days your old nature surges forward and you live in selfishness and self-gratification. Other days your new nature is at the forefront and you seek God's help and guidance throughout the day.

When those days happen, don't ever think that the battle is won. Living in obedience to God is a daily – no – minute-by-minute battle. Don't let your guard down. Stay close to God.

Pressure Cooker Living

*Though rulers sit together and slander me,
your servant will meditate on your decrees. Your
statutes are my delight; they are my counselors.*
Psalm 119:23-24

How good are you under pressure? How about peer pressure? When family members, coworkers or friends tease you because of your faith, what's your response? Do you keep on living for God and obeying Him because deep down inside that's who you are and you can't do anything less? Do you compromise what you know to be right and let their attitudes pull you away from obeying God? Where do you turn for strength in those times?

The best place, as the psalmist found, was God's Word. Don't be influenced by those who would pull you away from God. Meditate on His words and find strength in them.

Tough Love

*"You have heard that it was said,
'Love your neighbor and hate your
enemy.' But I tell you: Love your enemies
and pray for those who persecute you."*

Matthew 5:43-44

No one said that obeying God would be easy. Jesus confirms that in these verses. Anyone can love their friends. Friends are ... friends. You usually share similar values and morals. But enemies ... well, that's a whole different story. Especially enemies who make your life miserable.

Jesus said that the real mark of a believer, a person who lives out God's values, is that she loves her enemies and even prays for them. Tough call. But not impossible because God never asks us to do something without promising His strength to help. Just ask Him and perhaps some of those enemies will become friends.

Basic Obedience

"If my people, who are called by my name, will humble themselves and pray and seek my face and turn from their wicked ways, then will I hear from heaven and will forgive their sin and will heal their land."

2 Chronicles 7:14

This sounds so basic ... but it's so important. Four simple steps: Humble yourself (confess your sin and admit you need God's help). Pray (stay in communication with Him). Seek His face (take time to meditate and experience His presence). Turn from your sin (being in His presence must change you).

God promises to hear your prayers and to take action on your behalf. If you ever feel at a loss as to what obeying God means – start here.

Number One

"You shall have no other gods before me."
Exodus 20:3

Nothing should be more important to you than God. He won't stand for that. Is there something that is more important to you than God is? Think about it. You might not ever admit it out loud, but do you hold onto your children ... afraid of what God might require? Then they are before God in your heart.

What about your marriage, career, home, status in the community? What's important to you? Is there a secret compartment in your heart that only you and God know about, where you keep the something that is more precious to you than God Himself? This first of the Ten Commandments requires that nothing and no one be placed before God in your heart. Are you obeying Number One?

Living Together

You shall not murder ... commit adultery ...
steal ... give false testimony against
your neighbor ... covet your neighbor's
house ... wife ... manservant ... or
anything that belongs to your neighbor.
Exodus 20:13-17

The second half of the Ten Commandments gives clear guidelines for how to live with other people. Treating other people with respect is the foundation for obeying these commands. Of course, you would never murder or commit adultery, but what about the layers of behavior that lead to those actions – destroying someone's reputation by lying; cutting someone out of your life so that they are dead to you; lusting after another man?

Some of these sins are often found in our lives. Take an honest look at yourself. Do you need to clean anything up in your life?

Be Like Jesus

*Whoever claims to live in
him must walk as Jesus did.*
1 John 2:6

Jesus didn't come to earth just to die for our sins, though that gift is wonderful beyond understanding. He also came to show us how to live with one another. If we study His life we will learn how to live as His people in this world. We learn how to handle crisis situations by looking at His temptation or how He responded to those who questioned His authority. We learn about friendships by reading of how He interacted with His disciples and others. We learn about serving one another by reading of how He constantly gave of His time and energy to help other people.

We see how important Jesus felt it was for everyone to learn about God. When we study Jesus' life and try to live as He did, we will be living in obedience to God.

Active Love

*The entire law is summed up in a single
command: "Love your neighbor as yourself."*
Galatians 5:14

This verse cuts through all the garbage we sometimes produce in an effort to justify our actions and
attitudes, doesn't it? Loving your neighbor is the
clearest evidence that you are God's woman in this
world. Who is your neighbor? Remember the story
of the Good Samaritan (Luke 15)? Your neighbor
is anyone who has a need – even those who are
"different" from you. That means becoming aware
of and helping the undesirables, the unpopular, the
enemy.

Loving these people doesn't just mean sending
money to an organization to help them. It means
getting your hands dirty, opening your heart,
serving. Love them as much as you
love yourself – meet their needs as
quickly and thoroughly as you take
care of your own.

Know the Playbook

*Do not let this Book of the Law depart
from your mouth; meditate on it day and night,
so that you may be careful to do everything written
in it. Then you will be prosperous and successful.*

Joshua 1:8

A professional football player would no more go out on the field without studying his playbook than he would without his helmet and pads. He would be lost when a play was called because he wouldn't know what his responsibilities were in that play.

The Bible is our playbook. In it, God has outlined everything we need to know to live a life of obedience to Him. If we don't study it, then we won't know what we're supposed to do. Make time in your day ... every day ... to spend time in God's Word. The only way to obey it is to know what it says.

The Most Important

Above all else, guard your heart,
for it is the wellspring of life.
Proverbs 4:23

The writer of Proverbs has just spent 22 verses of this chapter on how to be wise and how to avoid pitfalls. When he comes to verse 23 he wants to make a point about how to avoid the bad choices of life. "Above all else" – more important than anything else I've just told you ... if you don't remember anything else I've said, remember this ... *guard your heart*. Be careful where you set your affections, watch what becomes important to you, mind your priorities.

Your heart determines the choices you make because it's very hard to go against what your heart is telling you. If you're serious about obeying God, put Him on the throne of your heart. Let Him determine your choices and the paths you follow.

Just Do It

Anyone, then, who knows the good he
ought to do and doesn't do it, sins.
James 4:17

There's no such thing as a spiritual gift of justification. Sin is sin. When you know something is wrong and you do it anyway … sin. Plain and simple. You can give a hundred reasons as to why you did it or how other people can do it and it's okay, but if God has told you in your heart that this is not right for you, then don't do it.

It also works the other way – when you know things you should do, but you refuse to do them … sin. Living a life of obedience to God means obeying all the information we have. So, when you stumble, confess, repent and move on. Don't fight the process by justifying your actions. You'll never make any progress that way. Learn and grow.

Drawing Card

You ought to live holy and godly lives as you look forward to the day of God and speed its coming.
2 Peter 3:11-12

Your goal in life should be to move toward becoming more and more godly. That means God's characteristics should be evident in your life ... to all people with whom you come into contact, not just your friends. Being godly is to be holy. Being holy is to stand out from the rest of the world by being moral, honest and loving.

You have a responsibility, as God's child and representative in this world, to know Him and live for Him so that people who aren't believers will be drawn to Him. Living a life of obedience to God's standards will set you apart from the world and they will see His love in you. That will draw them to Him.

Number One

"Love the Lord your God with all your heart and with all your soul and with all your mind. This is the first and greatest commandment. And the second is like it: Love your neighbor as yourself."
Matthew 22:37-39

Remember your first love? Remember how you were consumed by the object of your affections? You couldn't spend enough time with him or know too much about him. You wanted more than anything to please him. You wanted to know him so well that you could anticipate his needs and desires. Consuming love.

If we really loved God the way He wants us to, our love would be even more consuming than that first puppy love. Loving Him with all your heart, soul, and mind doesn't leave room for much else. What love energy is left goes out to our neighbors. Obeying God is loving. Loving is obeying God. Simple, isn't it?

Daily Test

Examine yourselves to see whether
you are in the faith; test yourselves.
2 Corinthians 13:5

Satan is sneaky. He doesn't generally get us off track by tossing major things in front of us. He usually wears us down in sneaky little ways. Like water wiggling into a crack in a rock and just pushing and pushing until the crack gets bigger and bigger, Satan picks away at our small weaknesses, making them larger and larger. Before we realize what is happening, he has subtly gained control of that area of our lives.

So, this is a timely reminder from Paul to test yourself … step back and examine your heart, your actions, your motivations … your obedience and see if you are where you should be. Don't let Satan wiggle in anywhere.

Falling

*If the LORD delights in a man's way, he makes
his steps firm; though he stumble, he will not
fall, for the LORD upholds him with his hand.*

Psalm 37:23-24

Can you imagine jumping out of an airplane and
freefalling for several hundred feet before opening
your parachute? Falling, falling, falling and praying
that the chute actually opens when you pull the cord.
Do you sometimes feel like you're falling in life?
You try to obey God, try to do the right things, but
you continually stumble. Sometimes you go down
and you're not sure how to get back up.

Rest assured that God sees when you're trying
to obey Him, He knows the desires of your heart.
He won't let you fall so far that you can't get back
up. The Lord Himself will hold you up with His
hand.

DECEMBER

Walking with God

Spiritually Fit

*Have nothing to do with godless myths and
old wives' tales; rather, train yourself to be
godly. For physical training is of some value, but
godliness has value for all things, holding promise
for both the present life and the life to come.*

1 Timothy 4:7-8

Every so often we become obsessed with getting
our physical bodies in shape, losing weight and
tightening muscles. But how much time do we
spend working on our spiritual lives? If you grew
up attending church, do you depend on what you
learned in your childhood to carry you through, or
are you constantly seeking to know more and more
about God? If you are newer to your faith – do you
hunger to know God's Word?

Each of us needs to study His Word on our own,
learning the truth of it and growing
more and more godly as we learn
to know Him better.

Watch Your Step

Blessed are they whose ways are blameless, who walk according to the law of the LORD. Blessed are they who keep his statutes and seek him with all their heart.

Psalm 119:1-2

Here's a call to look at your life honestly. You don't have to confess anything to anyone except God. Ask yourself this question – do you sometimes get lazy in your spiritual walk? After all, life is busy and demanding and there aren't enough hours in the day. It's so tempting to push aside things like prayer time or Bible study – promising yourself you'll get to it later – but sometimes later never comes.

The bottom line is that you will never grow in your walk with God, your faith will not become stronger and deeper, if you don't put some effort into it. Where you spend your time and energy is your choice – choose wisely!

War!

In my inner being I delight in God's law;
but I see another law at work in the members
of my body, waging war against the law
of my mind and making me a prisoner of
the law of sin at work within my members.

Romans 7:22-23

Obeying God is a constant struggle, isn't it? Satan fights against all efforts to know God and follow Him. He moves so quietly, planting thoughts and desires in your mind that wiggle and squirm, insisting on your attention. Paul accurately described this as a war being fought in our bodies. The only weapons we can use to fight this war are found in God's Word.

We cannot stand alone in these battles. We need the strength of God to help us stay constant. God's Word, prayer, accountability to Christian friends, listening for God's voice and guidance are the weapons that will help us win against Satan.

Growth Plates

Create in me a pure heart, O God,
and renew a steadfast spirit within me.
Psalm 51:10

The bottom line is that your spiritual walk will not grow unless you pray this prayer and mean it with all your heart. You cannot, by your own power and strength, make your heart pure. You can't stop your own sinfulness. As hard as you try, eventually the selfishness and evil in your heart will come through.

Only God can make your heart pure. Christ's sacrificial death made it possible for our hearts to be made pure. He took the punishment for your sin when He had never sinned. So, thank God that you have the opportunity to go deeper with Him – and ask Him to help you. Ask Him to purify your heart and to help you stand firm in your spirit.

Ask Him ... then let Him do it.

Standing Against Satan

Finally, be strong in the Lord and in his mighty power. Put on the full armor of God so that you can take your stand against the devil's schemes.

Ephesians 6:10-11

Life isn't easy. Every day brings new problems and temptations. You may find yourself getting weary because of the weight of the things you face day by day. Those are the times when Satan will wiggle his way into your life and quietly begin to turn you away from God. Don't let him! Stay close to God so that His strength and power can see you through the hard times.

Take full advantage of all the protection God offers through studying His Word, praying to Him, and becoming more and more like Him. These are the things that will help you stand strong against Satan.

Unworthy!

*O my God, I am too ashamed and
disgraced to lift up my face to you, my God,
because our sins are higher than our heads
and our guilt has reached to the heavens.*

Ezra 9:6

You can't grow stronger spiritually without first
recognizing the need to fall to your knees. You must
recognize the holiness and majesty of God and your
own unworthiness and sinfulness.

When you have grasped those two things, you
will begin to appreciate all that God has done for
you in making a way for you to enter His heaven.
Gratitude and praise will spill from you. More than
likely you will begin to hunger to know Him better
and better. Then, at that moment of recognizing
your weakness, you will begin to grow.

Praise Always!

Let everything that has breath
praise the LORD. Praise the LORD.
Psalm 150:6

This entire psalm is about praising God. The psalmist mentions some of His attributes – His power and greatness. It mentions some ways that He can be praised, such as with instruments and dancing. Then it almost seems as if the psalmist can no longer find the right words to express the powerful need to praise God. You can almost hear him shouting, "Let everything ... everything that breathes ... praise God!" That says it all. When your heart begins to understand God and fathom His greatness, His love, His power, His compassion, praise will simply spill from you. You won't be able to contain it!

Spend a few minutes meditating on God's love for you. Think about His faithfulness to you, His strength, His constancy. Do you feel like praising Him? Well, go right ahead!

Ready, Set, Grow!

If we claim to be without sin, we deceive ourselves and the truth is not in us. If we confess our sins, he is faithful and just and will forgive us our sins and purify us from all unrighteousness.
1 John 1:8-9

Spiritual growth won't happen unless you're honest with God and yourself. It's tempting to look at the evil in the world and justify your own sin. "Well, I'm not a murderer. I've never cheated on my taxes. I'm basically a good, honest person." That may be true ... but you're a good, honest person who is not without sin.

The first step in spiritual growth is recognizing and admitting to yourself that you sin ... every day. The next step is confessing that sin and asking God's forgiveness. Now your heart is a clean slate on which God can begin His amazing work.

Reward!

We who are still alive and are left will be caught up together with them in the clouds to meet the Lord in the air. And so we will be with the Lord forever.

1 Thessalonians 4:17

What a promise! Imagine that scene – believers everywhere being swooped up into the sky to meet Jesus Himself. Then they will go with Him to heaven … forever! This promise is good motivation to stay faithful to Him. We know this day is coming because God promised it.

Don't you want to stand before Him and hear Him say, "Well done, good and faithful servant"? Then continue growing stronger and more faithful in your walk with Him. And trust Him. Keep this image of meeting Jesus in your mind! What a celebration that will be!

A New Person

Put off your old self, which is being corrupted by its deceitful desires; to be made new in the attitude of your minds; and to put on the new self, created to be like God in true righteousness and holiness.

Ephesians 4:22-24

There are personal choices involved in living as a child of God. Every day you make the choice as to whether or not you will obey God.

To move forward in your spiritual growth, choose to put off your old self that is filled with selfishness and dishonesty and is more concerned about Number One than anyone else. Choose to put on the new self, the one that is like God and desires to serve Him. This new self is concerned about God first, others second and self last.

Trust and Obey

Trust in the LORD with all your heart
and lean not on your own understanding;
in all your ways acknowledge him
and he will make your paths straight.
Proverbs 3:5-6

These are powerful verses promising that God will direct your path. If you completely trust Him and don't try to run things yourself, He will guide your life. But this isn't a 40-60% deal. This verse says acknowledge God in *all* your ways.

You can't pick and choose certain parts of God's Word that you will obey while ignoring other areas. Give God control over your whole life … trust Him enough to believe that He will guide you and protect you. It's a comforting thought, isn't it, to know that He is in control? You don't have to worry about things. He already has it figured out!

Same, Same, Same

*Jesus Christ is the same yesterday
and today and forever.*
Hebrews 13:8

Have you ever known someone who was so moody that her personality seemed to drastically change from day to day or even hour to hour? You never knew which person was going to open the door on any given day. Some days she was Miss Sweet and Kind and some days she was the Evil Witch. That's something you never have to worry about with Jesus.

He never changes. He is the same today as He was a hundred years ago and that's the same way He will be a hundred years from now. You can count on Him always caring, always sacrificing, always teaching, always being the same. What a comfort!

Fooling No One

*I strive always to keep my conscience
clear before God and man.*
Acts 24:16

You can fool some of the people, some of the time.
You can say the Christian words, even quote Bible
verses. You can sing the old hymns of the faith and
the newest choruses. You can even pray and seem
to be lovingly concerned about others. But … you
can't fool God … ever! God looks at the heart so He
knows who you really are, down deep inside. The
only way to live before God is to keep your conscience clear.

Don't try to pretend you're something you're
not. Confess your shortcomings and ask Him to
help you not make the same mistake twice. Then
you can come before Him with a clear conscience,
knowing that He hears your prayers because He
loves you.

381

Owner's Manual

*All Scripture is God-breathed and is useful
for teaching, rebuking, correcting and training
in righteousness, so that the man of God may
be thoroughly equipped for every good work.*
2 Timothy 3:16-17

Scripture is pretty important. God uses it to teach and train us. He speaks to us through the words of Scripture. So, if we are going to grow stronger in our walk with Him, we'd better spend time studying and memorizing Scripture. By knowing His Word, we are equipped for whatever happens in life. Remember how Jesus quoted Scripture when He was tempted by Satan?

If it was important for Jesus to know the Words of Scripture, it must be very important for us, also. It's our "owner's manual" that will show us how to live this life in a way that honors and pleases God.

All the Way

*What does the LORD your God ask of you but to
fear the LORD your God, to walk in all his ways,
to love him, to serve the LORD your God with
all your heart and with all your soul, and
to observe the LORD's commands and decrees.*

Deuteronomy 10:12-13

We may be guilty today, at least in some ways, of treating God too much like our buddy or friend. By doing that, we do not fear Him and hold Him in awe as we should. God demands our respect. He is powerful, mighty, and jealous for our worship.

It is a privilege to be able to serve and obey Him. However, He doesn't want half-hearted service. He wants everything we can give. The two things go together – if we fear and revere Him, we will desire to serve and obey Him completely and be honored at the privilege of doing so.

Live and Learn

*It is God who works in you to will
and to act according to his good purpose.*
Philippians 2:13

Be encouraged because God is at work in your life.
The stuff you're going through – problems, trials,
disappointments, victories, joys, celebrations – are
things you can learn from. God doesn't put problems
in your life and He doesn't always take them away,
no matter how hard you pray. But He will walk
with you through them and help you learn valuable
lessons from each situation.

God is concerned about how much you grow in
your faith and trust. So when you experience difficult
times, look for lessons you can learn to make you
stronger. When things are going well in your life,
continue to look for what you can learn.

Perspective

"Seek first his kingdom and his righteousness,
and all these things will be given to you as well."
Matthew 6:33

This statement comes in the middle of one of Jesus' sermons. He has just been telling His listeners that worry is pointless and unnecessary. He teaches that God can be trusted to take care of everything, and we can't change anything by worrying anyway.

Here, Jesus is saying, "Get your life in perspective." What is truly important is that you learn more and more about God and how He wants you to live. If you focus your energy on that and don't worry so much about the day to day stuff, you will realize that God takes care of all that anyway.

Anonymity

*"Be careful not to do your acts of righteousness
before men, to be seen by them. If you do, you
will have no reward from your Father in heaven."*
Matthew 6:1

Everyone likes to look good. Once in a while a little pat on the back or a "You're a good person" comment feels good. It's encouraging. But if the only reason you do good things is so others will praise you, your motivation is all wrong. Caring for others should show them the love of God.

You are God's hands in this world and can show His heart to those who don't know Him. It is better to do acts of righteousness anonymously or quietly so that God is the only one glorified. When you can do that, God sees that your heart desires to honor Him and have Him lifted up, not yourself. Then your reward from Him is sure.

Freedom

It is for freedom then that Christ has set us free. Stand firm, then, and do not let yourselves be burdened again by a yoke of slavery.

Galatians 5:1

Christ's work on the cross set you free. He died so you can live. Once you've taken hold of that fact and accepted Him as Savior, your life begins to change. The freedom Christ gives opens your eyes to His love. It teaches you how to live in this world, obeying God and honoring Him. What a privilege!

Of course, Satan is going to fight this freedom with all his power. He wants you back in that yoke of slavery. That's when the standing firm comes in. Stand firm against sliding back to where you used to be. Stay close to God and don't let Satan pull you back.

Good Citizenship

*Remind the people to be subject to rulers
and authorities, to be obedient, to be
ready to do whatever is good, to slander
no one, to be peaceable and considerate,
and to show true humility toward all men.*
Titus 3:1-2

Remember that you are Christ's hands and feet in
this world. Some people may never enter a church
or hear a sermon, so they only know what God is
like by the way you live your life. Being a good
and responsible citizen is part of your spiritual
walk.

It is important that you obey the laws and be
kind and peaceable. If something should happen
where the government asks you to do something
that you believe contradicts the Bible, then your
protests should be peaceful and within
the law. Remember that all you do
is a reflection of your Christian
walk.

Hear and Act

*Do not merely listen to the word,
and so deceive yourselves. Do what it says.*
James 1:22

Studying God's Word is important to spiritual growth. When you spend time reading His Word, He will begin to help you understand the depths of its meaning. That understanding prompts (and demands) action. There should begin to be changes in your behavior and attitudes.

The goal of the spiritual walk is to become more like Christ. If you don't see that happening in your life – and if others don't see you changing – then you may be deceiving yourself in some ways. Be honest with yourself regarding how serious you are about your spiritual walk and whether you are allowing God to change and grow your heart.

Thankfulness, No Matter What

*Give thanks to the LORD, for he
is good. His love endures forever.*
Psalm 136:1

This entire psalm offers praise to God. When your eyes and heart are opened to God – to His strength, power, love, justice and creativity – praise bursts forth. The real test of your praise comes when life isn't going so well. When you're struggling with trials, as the psalmists so often did, can you still praise God? In the middle of the "stuff" of life, can your heart remember who God is? Can you hang on to that memory and praise Him, even when you can't see His hand at work in your life at that very moment?

That's real praise – trusting His heart even when you can't see His hand – because that shows that you understand His presence with you is constant and His love for you is true.

Strong Trust

Trust in the LORD forever, for the
LORD, the LORD, is the Rock eternal.
Isaiah 26:4

Trust is easy when things are going well, right? When finances are secure, health is good, relationships are cruising, children obeying, trusting is a breeze. But what happens when any one of those elements takes a serious knock? Can you still trust God when you don't know how the mortgage is going to be paid? Is your faith strong when there is a serious health threat to you or someone you love? Knowing that God is your Rock can only be learned through the trials of life. You don't need a Rock when things are going well.

When (not if) you face times of crisis, trust God to see you through. Believe that He is walking with you and He can see what's up ahead. Hold on to Him. Let Him be your Rock.

Purposeful Living

*If you have any encouragement from being
united with Christ, if any comfort from his
love, if any fellowship with the Spirit, if any
tenderness and compassion, then make my joy
complete by being like-minded, having the
same love, being one in spirit and purpose.*

Philippians 2:1-2

Christ's church is made up of people who are bound
together by their common elder brother – Christ.
Members of a family should love one another, quirks
and all. Paul knew that sometimes that's difficult,
but he also knew that it's important.

We should be filled with love for Christ and
be united in the purpose of sharing Him with
those who haven't met Him yet. We won't fulfill
that purpose if we get sidetracked with family
squabbles. If you're struggling in your relationship
with someone, settle it … in love. Then, purposefully
go about the work of sharing Christ through your
words and your life.

A Good Mystery

*My purpose is that they may be encouraged
in heart and united in love, so that they may
have the full riches of complete understanding,
in order that they may know the mystery of
God, namely, Christ, in whom are hidden
all the treasures of wisdom and knowledge.*

Colossians 2:2-3

Paul cared about other believers and wanted them to understand the possibilities of life in Christ. Paul made a good point – that to know the fullness of the riches of God available through Christ, we need to be united in love with people around us.

The better we know Christ, the more we understand about God and His wisdom and knowledge. So, take this as encouragement to get along with others, be encouraged and encouraging, and seek to unravel the mystery of God by knowing Christ.

A Shining Light

*"You are the light of the world. A city on a
hill cannot be hidden ... Let your light
shine before men that they may see your good
deeds and praise your Father in heaven."*
Matthew 5:14, 16

Jesus doesn't say that you might be the light. He says
you *are* the light. You have the incredible privilege
of being filled with God's presence. Sometimes it
takes courage to take a stand and be open about your
faith in God, letting others see your light shine.

You don't have to be obnoxiously pushy about
your faith. In fact you shouldn't be. Your light shines
in the way you live your life, day in and day out.
Your actions and reactions show what you believe
more than your words do. Let your light shine so
that those around you can see your Father in
heaven.

Comfort in Trouble

*The LORD is my shepherd, I shall not be in want ...
Even though I walk through the valley of the
shadow of death, I will fear no evil, for you are
with me; your rod and your staff they comfort me.*

Psalm 23:1, 4

God will take care of you ... no matter what. His presence will surround you even in the most painful times of life. He doesn't promise to take away the pain or difficulty, but He promises that you will never walk alone through them. There is no reason to be afraid, even when facing death, because God has provided the means for comfort.

It's important that you begin spending time with God on a daily basis, laying the foundation of trust and knowledge of His Word so your heart believes you can trust Him when the rough times come.

Rock Solid

"Heaven and earth will pass away,
but my words will never pass away."
Mark 13:31

How do you spend the bulk of your time? If you wrote down everything you have done in the past week, where would it show that your priorities are? The "urgent" things in life demand our time, attention and energy so that the truly important things get pushed aside.

Jesus said that everything in life is going to pass away – every one of those "urgent" things that you give so much time and energy to. However, His Word will never pass away. Spending time reading and understanding His Word might be important then, don't you think? Do you need to make time in your life to have a daily quiet time ... time to read God's Word and let it sink into your heart? It's important.

Total Love

But God demonstrates his own love for us in this:
While we were still sinners, Christ died for us.

Romans 5:8

God loves you. When you stop and think about it, that's incredible. God, who created all that is, who has power and strength that cannot be equaled ... loves you. He showed that love in such an undeniable way when Christ died for you.

As you seek to grow stronger in your spiritual walk, let your mind focus on your own sinfulness ... no one knows it better than you do ... then spend some time meditating on Christ's sacrifice for you. He couldn't have shown His love any more completely. He couldn't have given any more. Think about how much He loves you. If you can, just let it sink into your heart. How will you respond to that love?

A New Person

Therefore, if anyone is in Christ, he is a new creation; the old has gone, the new has come.
2 Corinthians 5:17

Where have you come from? The person you were before Christ came into your life should be gone. The habits and attitudes that defined you then should be changed. You are a new creature. A door has opened in your heart that Christ walked through, bringing love, compassion, concern for others, honesty, justice, and self-sacrifice with it. Every characteristic that defines Christ can now define you. The struggle is to keep that old person, with all her old habits and attitudes, away. Old habits die hard.

Begin each day by asking the Lord to help the new person shine over the old person. Ask Him to shine through you so the new is shining through and the old is gone.

Daily Walk

And now, dear children, continue in him,
so that when he appears we may be confident
and unashamed before him at his coming.
1 John 2:28

Don't let up. Satan continually attempts to wiggle his way into your life. He wants you to stop trying to live for God. He doesn't want you to study God's Word or to pray. He wants you to be lukewarm and discouraged. Don't let him do that to you.

To continue in Christ means to know Him in your daily life. Spend time with Him each day, let your habits reflect how He lived and loved on this earth. Make it your goal that every day, not just on your good days, but every day Christ would be evident in your life. Let Him love others through you. Serve others with the humility Christ showed to all.